Adams

The Professional COUNSELOR

Competencies, Performance Guidelines and Assessment

2nd Edition

Edited by

DENNIS W. ENGELS, Ph.D.

JOSEPH D. DAMERON, Ed.D.

Written by faculty members of the
Department of Counselor Education
University of North Texas, Denton, Texas

American Association for
Counseling and Development
5999 Stevenson Avenue, Alexandria, VA 22304

American Association for Counseling and Development
5999 Stevenson Avenue
Alexandria, VA 22304

Cover design by Sarah Jane Valdez

Library of Congress Cataloging-in-Publication Data

The Professional counselor: competencies, performance, guidelines, and assessment / edited by Dennis W. Engels and Joseph D. Dameron. —2nd ed.
p. cm.
Includes bibliographical references.
ISBN 1-55620-075-7
1. Counseling—Evaluation. 2. Counselors—Rating of.
I. Engels, Dennis W. II. Dameron, Joseph D.
BF637.C6P78 1990
361.3'23—dc20 90–39374
CIP

Printed in the United States of America

CONTENTS

FOREWORD

The counseling profession has come a long way in establishing standards for preparation through the combined efforts of the American Association for Counselor Education and Supervision (ACES), the American College Personnel Association (ACPA), the Council for the Advancement of Standards for Student Services/Development Programs (CAS), the American Association for Counseling and Development (AACD, formerly APGA) and the Council for Accreditation of Counseling and Related Educational Programs (CACREP). In addition, such bodies as the National Board for Certified Counselors (NBCC) and its specialties, along with the National Academy of Certified Clinical Mental Health Counselors (NACCMHC), have provided opportunities for practitioners to demonstrate and update their knowledge as trends in the field and in society dictate.

As we know, knowledge changes, new areas of knowledge emerge, and new ways of obtaining that knowledge are identified. Since this manual was first published in 1980, major changes have occurred in the counseling profession, in the populations we serve, and in social, political, economic, and educational contexts. It is appropriate that, after a decade, our views of "the professional counselor" should be reexamined.

As we look to 1994, the CACREP standards for accreditation of counselor preparation programs again will be refined and revised. This handbook, which draws heavily from the CACREP standards framework, will probably be ready for another revision some time before the next decade, as must happen if we are to incorporate the changes necessary in an increasingly global and diverse society. These changes have and will continue to have an impact on what we do to deliver services to clients and students in a variety of settings and how we decide what knowledge is worth knowing and sharing.

It is important for professional counselors to have guidelines for preparation standards as well as for assessing their own professional development. To be a professional counselor today requires competencies in a number of areas, including the traditional areas of individual and group counseling, career development, appraisal and testing, and clinical skills, and newer areas such as social and cultural issues, professional ethics, supervision, and program development and management.

With the increasing focus on developmental competencies in our profession, it becomes essential to provide specific, updated guidelines in the core areas of entry-level counselor preparation. *The Professional Counselor* is ideal for use along with regular counselor education texts. While retaining the original publication's format, such as the competence assessment scale and the updated chapters on personality characteristics—program development, school counseling, and other areas—the text also adds important new concepts in such areas as addictions, multicultural and specific populations, and marriage and family.

Use of the term *specific populations* rather than *special populations* to address competencies related to race, gender, ethnicity, sexual orientation, age, and disability communicates attention to unique differences in a positive way without implying that most of our literature is addressed to generic populations. Clearly the chapter titles reflect a close relationship to the current "state of the art" in 1990. For counselors trained under earlier models, the manual offers baseline data for examining what they know and do not know.

The competencies incorporated into this publication are worded in ways that can be measured. They also reflect the terminology of the current CACREP standards, as well as other competence standards, such as those for career development, supervision, and ethics. The format provides for statements of general competencies accompanied by performance guidelines.

The 13-member faculty of the Department of Counselor Education at the University of North Texas has provided a positive model of collaboration in putting this revised publication together, guided by co-editors Dennis Engels and Joseph Dameron. They also have prepared a needed model for accountability, a window from which to assess the behavior and skills of counselors, and an updated and extensive list of selected readings.

This publication is appropriately labeled a manual. As such, it should be very useful to counselor educators, counselors, and other professionals who want a snapshot of the knowledge, skills, and characteristics that describe a professional counselor in the 1990s. Although we recognize that our profession encompasses counseling **and human development**, the primary focus of this work is on counseling, with some implicit and explicit attention to human development. We hope that, along with professional accreditation standards, it will provide an updated framework for describing, examining, assessing, developing, and refining what is needed for professional counselors to function effectively in this changing society.

Sunny Hansen, President
American Association for
Counseling and Development
1989–90

AUTHORS

Faculty of the Department of Counselor Education, College of Education, University of North Texas, Denton, Texas:

DENNIS W. ENGELS (EDITOR), PhD, LPC, NCC, NCCC, is professor of counselor education and student services administration. Dr. Engels has held offices in state and national professional counseling associations, has served as consulting editor on nationally refereed journals, has numerous publications, and has worked and consulted with public and private sector organizations and agencies throughout the United States.

JOSEPH D. DAMERON (EDITOR), EdD, LPC, NCC, is professor of counselor education and student services administration. Dr. Dameron has served twice as president of the Texas Association for Counseling and Development and is presently serving on the board of this association.

ROBERT C. BERG, EdD, licensed psychologist, LPC, professor of counselor education and student services administration

CYNTHIA K. CHANDLER, EdD, LPC, assistant professor of counselor education and student services administration

MARTIN J. GIEDA, PhD, licensed psychologist, NCC, CRC, assistant professor of counselor education and student services administration

RILEY L. HARVILL, EdD, LPC, associate professor of counselor education and student services administration

JOHN L. HIPPLE, PhD, LPC, associate professor of counselor education and student services administration

JANICE MINOR HOLDEN, EdD, LPC, NCC, ACST, assistant professor of counselor education and student services administration

TERRY KOTTMAN, PhD, LPC, NCC, assistant professor of counselor education and student services administration

GARRY L. LANDRETH, EdD, licensed psychologist, LPC, professor of counselor education and student services administration

BYRON W. MEDLER, EdD, licensed psychologist, LPC, NCC, professor of counselor education and student services administration

E. DOUGLAS NORTON, PhD, LPC, NCC, associate professor of counselor education and student services administration

BOBBIE L. WILBORN, PhD, licensed psychologist, LPC, NCC, department chair, and professor of counselor education and student services administration

AUTHORS

PREFACE

This revision has been prepared for counselors, counselor educators, supervisors, aspiring counselors, and paraprofessionals who are interested in examining and implementing competency-based approaches to counselor preparation, practice, and evaluation. The book's format makes it suitable for use as a textbook in that general competencies are listed adjacent to specific performance guidelines and an assessment scale for each of the performance guidelines. In addition to its preservice utility, the book should also continue to serve as a focused stimulus for in-service workshops and individual uses.

CONTENT

Content of this revision differs significantly from previous works in several ways, but the overall content mix remains highly similar, with attention to competencies (and guidelines) that reflect national accreditation standards, state and national credentialing standards, and competency and credentialing standards of national counseling and development organizations. Individual chapters focus on knowledge and skills related to specific settings such as schools, mental health agencies, and universities, and generic or core curriculum elements such as human growth and development, helping relationships, and professional orientation. Attention to ethics has been infused throughout each chapter of the book to underscore the pervasive importance of professional ethics. Chapter contents are as follows:

"Assessment of Competencies of Professional Counselors" introduces an evaluation schematic for use throughout the text.

Chapter 1, "Personality Characteristics of Professional Counselors," has been refined and expanded to include several new concepts, such as self-discipline and personal responsibility.

Chapter 2, "Counseling Competencies for Selected Environments and Populations," has been expanded to include counseling competencies related to Environments and Specialties and Common-Core elements covered by the Council for the Accreditation of Counseling and Related Educational Programs (CACREP) standards. Subchapter 2A, "Addiction Counseling," was added because this topic seems pertinent for counselors in almost every setting. Other subchapters focus on selected populations: subchapter 3B, "Child and Adolescent Counseling," subchapter 3H, "Multicultural and Specific Populations Counseling," and subchapter 3G, "Marriage, Family, and Relationship Counseling."

Chapter 3, "Program Planning, Development, and Administration Competencies," combines and refines the contents of the two chapters previously entitled "Coordination Competencies" and "Planning and Development Competencies" in the first edition. The logical relationship and progression of these competencies lend themselves to this new configuration. The dominant focus of this chapter is on providing developmental programs, with some attention to programming for and addressing crises.

Chapter 4, "Life-Style and Career Development Competencies," encompasses the chapters originally entitled "Career Development Competencies" and "Placement and Follow-Up Competencies." These topics lend themselves to condensation and combination, reflecting a fuller competency continuum without sacrificing substantive coverage of the topics. In this chapter, every effort was made to reflect the National Career Development Association's (1990) current attention to credentialing and standards and *The National Career Development Guidelines* of the National Occupational Information Coordinating Committee (NOICC) (1989) as well as other pertinent sources.

Chapter 5, "Appraisal Competencies," replaces the original title, "Measurement and Evaluation Competencies," in a further effort to reflect terminology from the CACREP standards. This chapter covers appraisal and assessment issues, knowledge, and skills.

Chapter 6, "Diagnosis, Record-Keeping, and Referral Competencies," brings new dimensions into the narrative that are essential for counselors, especially licensed counselors, in most settings.

Chapter 7, "Counselor Supervision Competencies," covers an area of great importance in the growing emphasis on professional credentialing and continuing education. Every effort has been made to incorporate recent and current work of the Association for Counselor Education and Supervision (ACES) and other state and national entities in this area.

Chapter 8, "Consultation Competencies," has been updated through modest changes to reflect current practice.

Chapter 9, "Research and Evaluation Competencies," was updated with attention to process and outcome research, evaluation, human subjects, and related issues and competencies.

The bibliography, **Selected Readings**, has been updated and expanded to include current and landmark reading suggestions for all topics covered in the 9 chapters.

INFUSION

As noted at various points above, each chapter also includes, as appropriate, specific attention to the following areas and topics: at-risk populations; computer-based/electronic systems; ethics; gender; human growth and development; law; social and cultural foundations; professional orientation; and helping relationships. This infusion highlights ethical and legal issues in every chapter, with special attention to the 1988 American Association for Counseling and Development (AACD) *Ethical Standards.*

CHAPTER FORMATS

Chapter formats resemble those of the first edition, but also include attention to each of the specific "knowledge and skill competence areas" (p. 25) of the eight areas of the Curriculum Common-Core, as listed on pages 25 through 27 of the *Accreditation Procedures Manual and Application* (CACREP, 1988). CACREP Common-Core Curriculum elements 1. "Human Growth and Development," 2. "Social and Cultural Foundations," 3. "Helping Relationships," and 8. "Professional Orientation," (CACREP, 1988, pp. 25–27) are infused within the narratives of various chapters and subchapters. Competencies for the four remaining curriculum core areas are designated as separate chapters or subchapters in the table of contents as follows: subchapter 2D, "Group Counseling," chapter 4, "Life-Style and Career Development Competencies," chapter 5, "Appraisal Competencies," and chapter 9, "Research and Evaluation Competencies."

Chapter 4, "Life-Style and Career Development Competencies," focuses on Curriculum Core Area 5 (Life-Style and Career Development), including all study areas listed under that core area (5a–j) on page 26 of the 1988 CACREP Manual. This focus supplements coverage of other appropriate areas such as those reflected in the 1990 draft of the NCDA professional standards committee report (NCDA, 1990) and related topics, for example, facilitation of career decision making. Likewise, subchapter 2D, "Group Counseling," includes all five study areas (4a–e) listed under the "Group" common core area (CACREP, 1988, p. 26), and draws upon organizational position papers. In these examples and throughout the book, every effort was exerted to include current information from all pertinent sources, especially AACD Divisions, The National Board for Certified Counselors (NBCC), and CACREP, as well as long-standing fundamentals.

The four CACREP Environmental designations for counselor preparation programs are reflected throughout the document. The Environmental and Specialty Standards are covered in chapter 2 as follows: Subchapter 2C, "Community and Mental Health Counseling," combines the counseling competencies of the first two Environmental Standards; subchapter 2E, "Higher Education Counseling" addresses counseling competencies related to Student Affairs Practice in Higher Education; and the counseling competencies of the final CACREP Environmental Standard are covered in subchapter 2I, "School Counseling." Additionally, attention to setting specific and related environmental and specialty standards is infused throughout the balance of the work.

ISSUES

As this manuscript goes to press, there is considerable debate throughout the American Association for Counseling and Development (AACD) regarding an operational definition of the term *professional*. Much of the discussion seems focused on whether membership in AACD (and, hence, professional status) should be inclusive (open to many from various backgrounds) or exclusive (limited). Inclusivity and exclusivity discussions have focused primarily on what formal educational level and major should be required for membership. Although the authors acknowledge the importance of these and similar discussions in the larger aspect of professional development, they see a need for ideals, standards, and competencies for helping professionals and paraprofessionals in all settings. Hence, the standards presented in this work are meant for use by all who work to facilitate human growth and development. Moreover, although this work is obviously aimed at professional counselors and counseling supervisors, the respective goal statements preceding each listing of competencies and performance guidelines are written to allow for and encourage use by all professionals, aspiring professionals, and paraprofessionals. This is done to enhance and encourage fuller professional awareness and development in order to foster more effective counseling and development of all populations served by counselors and helping paraprofessionals.

Since the first edition, great changes have occurred in the area of credentialing, especially in terms of counselor certification and licensure. James Muro, 1980 ACES President, noted in his preface to the original work that accreditation would be an essential underpinning for credentialing efforts to succeed. Ironically, the pace of program accreditation has been decidedly slower than the rapid proliferation of state credentialing and licensure acts. Over 30 states have counselor licensure, and NBCC is a viable force. State legislators have not required accreditation as the cornerstone it was hailed to be, and only 65 of more than 400 counselor preparation programs have CACREP accredited programs. Nevertheless, much of the revision of this work has centered on the CACREP standards as a means of highlighting and promoting the standards among counselors, supervisors, and counselor educators in the larger hope that increased familiarity with the standards will help inform and focus the debate and action that will shape the future of professional credentialing and standards.

A CAUTION

Two disclaimers are in order regarding this publication. First, the competencies listed in this work are not exhaustive of all competencies either needed by or required of professional counselors. Rather, the approach has been to specify major competencies and performance guidelines while also providing additional attention to competencies through the "Selected Readings" section. Second, just as no one in today's information society can know everything worth knowing in any professional field, no professional counselor can be fully competent in all areas presented here. Rather, we have provided criteria for counselors and others to use as one means of operationally defining professional counseling according to competencies.

SUMMARY

This revision has been substantial. The main purpose of the work is to specify major competencies and performance guidelines for a variety of uses by counselors, human services professionals, and others interested in the helping and human development professions. Accordingly, the evaluation schematic is designed for individualized interpretation by counselors, counselor educators, and counseling supervisors as one basis for assessing competence in the preparation, continuing education, and supervision of counselors and prospective counselors.

—*Dennis W. Engels*
Joseph D. Dameron

REFERENCES

American Association for Counseling and Development. (1988). *Ethical standards.* Alexandria, VA: Author.

Council for Accreditation of Counseling and Related Educational Programs. (1988). *Accreditation procedures manual and application.* Alexandria, VA: Author.

National Career Development Association. Professional Standards Committee. (1990, March). *Career counseling standards* (Draft). Alexandria, VA: NCDA.

National Occupational Information Coordinating Committee. (1989). *National career development guidelines.* Washington, DC: Author.

ASSESSMENT OF COMPETENCIES OF PROFESSIONAL COUNSELORS: AN EVALUATION SCHEMATIC

When using the columns located in the "Assessment" section of this manual, the following key is recommended:

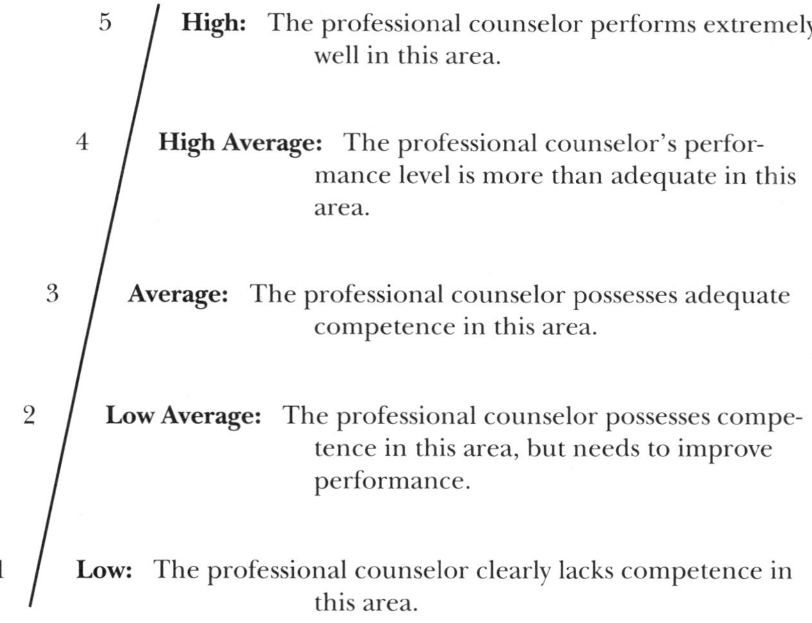

5 **High:** The professional counselor performs extremely well in this area.
4 **High Average:** The professional counselor's performance level is more than adequate in this area.
3 **Average:** The professional counselor possesses adequate competence in this area.
2 **Low Average:** The professional counselor possesses competence in this area, but needs to improve performance.
1 **Low:** The professional counselor clearly lacks competence in this area.

NO = **No opportunity to assess:** The professional counselor has not performed or has not been provided an opportunity to perform in this competence area.

NE = **Not essential to assessment:** The professional counselor does not consider that the competence statement, guideline, or both are requisite to counseling performance.

CHAPTER 1

PERSONALITY CHARACTERISTICS OF PROFESSIONAL COUNSELORS

GOAL STATEMENT: The professional counselor possesses personality characteristics that enable him or her to establish and maintain a therapeutic relationship with clients and to facilitate clients' constructive change process.

COMPETENCIES **The counselor is a skilled professional who is able to:**	PERFORMANCE GUIDELINES **The professional counselor provides evidence of competence by demonstrating the ability to:**		ASSESSMENT	Low 1	2	Average 3	4	High 5	NO	NE
1. Be committed to the welfare of others.	1.1	Put aside personal concerns during counseling sessions in order to focus on client concerns.	1.1							
	1.2	Nonverbally and verbally communicate a genuine interest in and caring for clients.	1.2							
	1.3	Verbalize a primary commitment to assist clients and to act in their best interest.	1.3							
2. Be sensitive to others.	2.1	Be emotionally affected or touched by the experiences and feelings of clients.	2.1							
	2.2	Show awareness of a broad range of client feelings, thoughts, values, and attitudes.	2.2							
	2.3	Identify the expectations of clients, coworkers, and supervisors.	2.3							

				1	2	3	4	5		NO	NE
				Low		Average		High			
3. Be empathic.	3.1	Communicate an understanding of each client's world as perceived by the client.	3.1								
	3.2	Formulate verbal responses that accurately and concisely reflect the content and feeling of clients' verbal and nonverbal messages.	3.2								
	3.3	Avoid ridicule, destructive criticism, and passive hostility in interactions with clients.	3.3								
4. Respect individuality.	4.1	Recognize and show acceptance of differences between the counselor's and client's subjective experiences and viewpoints.	4.1								
	4.2	Remain objective toward client opinions, practices, values, and emotional reactions that differ from those of the counselor.	4.2								
	4.3	Avoid the imposition of personal values on the client.	4.3								
	4.4	Exhibit a reasonable absence of prejudicial attitudes and stereotypical thinking.	4.4								
	4.5	Counsel clients of both genders and from various socioeconomic, cultural, and racial groups.	4.5								

COMPETENCIES The counselor is a skilled professional who is able to:	PERFORMANCE GUIDELINES The professional counselor provides evidence of competence by demonstrating the ability to:		ASSESSMENT	Low 1	2	Average 3	4	High 5	NO	NE
5. Believe in the positive potential of people.	5.1	Verbally and nonverbally communicate a perception of clients as worthy and responsible.	5.1							
	5.2	Communicate hope; express belief in clients' capacity to solve problems, manage their lives, and grow.	5.2							
6. Be self-aware and self-accepting.	6.1	Express a clear understanding of personal needs, values, strengths, weaknesses, feelings, and motivations that may impinge upon effectiveness as a counselor.	6.1							
	6.2	Experience self as a person of worth, dignity, and self-sufficiency.	6.2							
	6.3	Recognize and appropriately meet personal needs: physical, psychological, social, and spiritual.	6.3							
	6.4	Identify self-expectations.	6.4							
7. Systematically conceptualize human behavior and the process of change.	7.1	Interview clients using direct and indirect methods of inquiry, ranging from casual conversation to structured diagnostic assessment.	7.1							
	7.2	Apply theoretical constructs to determine the meaning of specific human problems.	7.2							

				1	2	3	4	5	NO	NE
	7.3	Use knowledge of human behavior and counseling theory to generate appropriate counseling goal(s) and modality of treatment.	7.3							
	7.4	Modify specific interventions on the basis of effectiveness.	7.4							
8. Facilitate personal development in others.	8.1	Recognize appropriate levels of counselor and client responsibility for the counseling process and act on that recognition.	8.1							
	8.2	Allow the client to initiate appropriate leading during counseling sessions.	8.2							
	8.3	Facilitate client expression and self-exploration.	8.3							
	8.4	Explore with the client rather than for the client.	8.4							
	8.5	Communicate a belief in clients' ability to think, feel or act differently than they have in the past.	8.5							
	8.6	Respond appropriately and with immediacy to important material as it arises in the counseling session.	8.6							
				Low		Average		High		

COMPETENCIES The counselor is a skilled professional who is able to:	PERFORMANCE GUIDELINES The professional counselor provides evidence of competence by demonstrating the ability to:		ASSESSMENT	Low 1	2	Average 3	4	High 5	NO	NE
(Continued) 8. Facilitate personal development in others.	8.7	Point out how clients have been restricted or have restricted themselves in the past, and present possible alternatives for the present and future.	8.7							
	8.8	Verbally and nonverbally encourage clients to choose constructive behavior and discourage clients from choosing destructive behavior.	8.8							
	8.9	Support clients' efforts to cope and change, and confront client discrepancies, in proportions appropriate to each individual client.	8.9							
	8.10	Verbally identify small increments of change and integrate them into an overall pattern or theme within the counseling process.	8.10							
9. Have a high tolerance for stress and frustration.	9.1	Maintain equanimity during times of stress and discomfort, both one's own and the client's.	9.1							
	9.2	Exhibit calm and persistent courage in the face of trying circumstances.	9.2							

				1	2	3	4	5	NO	NE
	9.3	Exhibit patience with each client's pace of change rather than attempt to hurry or force change.	9.3							
10. Respect freedom of choice.	10.1	Use the counseling process to enhance client freedom rather than control.	10.1							
	10.2	Communicate verbally and nonverbally to the client the freedom to retain cherished values, but point to the undesirability of retaining self-defeating thoughts and behaviors.	10.2							
11. Communicate effectively.	11.1	Communicate in specific and concrete, rather than general and abstract, terms.	11.1							
	11.2	Communicate in a style compatible with the communication style and developmental level of the client.	11.2							
	11.3	Openly communicate a wide range of affective experiences, from genuine anger to spontaneous tenderness and caring.	11.3							
	11.4	Clearly communicate ideas and concepts relevant to the counseling process.	11.4							
	11.5	Demonstrate congruence between verbal and nonverbal behavior.	11.5							
	11.6	Time and frame communication in ways that promote therapeutic goals.	11.6							
				Low		Average		High		

COMPETENCIES The counselor is a skilled professional who is able to:	PERFORMANCE GUIDELINES The professional counselor provides evidence of competence by demonstrating the ability to:		ASSESSMENT	Low 1	2	Average 3	4	High 5	NO	NE
12. Be creative.	12.1	Spontaneously use and/or create interventions, consistent with the counselor's guiding theory, that facilitate the client's exploration and/or growth.	12.1							
	12.2	Utilize clients' fantasies, metaphors, and imagery to enhance the therapeutic process.	12.2							
	12.3	Take appropriate risks and be vulnerable.	12.3							
13. Possess a sense of humor.	13.1	Laugh at self when appropriate.	13.1							
	13.2	Laugh appropriately with clients out of an appreciation for what clients are experiencing.	13.2							
	13.3	Take a humorous approach when appropriate.	13.3							
14. Maintain objectivity.	14.1	Avoid becoming overly involved in the problems of clients and others.	14.1							
	14.2	Remain open to and facilitate clients' intense affective responses, including those directed toward the counselor.	14.2							
15. Exercise self-discipline.	15.1	Effectively manage personal assets (e.g., knowledge, skills, energy, time).	15.1							

				1	2	3	4	5		NO	NE
	15.2	Interact with others in an assertive manner that evidences emotional awareness, emotional control, and mutual respect.	15.2								
	15.3	Work as a team player in cooperation with professional and paraprofessional colleagues.	15.3								
16. Be committed to professional growth.	16.1	Maintain active membership in professional organizations (e.g., AACD, state ACD organizations, other organizations related to areas of specialization).	16.1								
	16.2	Appropriately receive and use feedback, both positive and negative, from clients, supervisors, and professional peers.	16.2								
	16.3	Offer appropriate feedback, both positive and negative, to peers and supervisors.	16.3								
	16.4	Apply an awareness of current social, legal, and economic trends in the counseling process.	16.4								
	16.5	Pursue continuing education to better meet the needs of clients (e.g., attend professional conferences and workshops, keep current with the professional literature, periodically seek continuing supervision).	16.5								
				Low		Average		High			

COMPETENCIES The counselor is a skilled professional who is able to:	PERFORMANCE GUIDELINES The professional counselor provides evidence of competence by demonstrating the ability to:		ASSESSMENT	Low 1	2	Average 3	4	High 5	NO	NE
(Continued) 16. Be committed to professional growth.	16.6	Reassess existing beliefs in light of new information.	16.6							
17. Recognize and respond appropriately to personal and professional abilities and limitations.	17.1	Specify personal and professional qualifications and offer only those services for which the counselor is qualified.	17.1							
	17.2	Communicate to the client the nature of the counseling relationship so that the client understands the limits of the services offered.	17.2							
	17.3	Formulate verbal and written statements of personal and role limits that are consistent with the setting, the level of professional training and personal development, and the consensual opinions of other qualified professionals.	17.3							
	17.4	Communicate that the client will be assisted in finding appropriate sources of help when personal or institutional limits are exceeded.	17.4							
	17.5	Refer clients when necessary, based on an awareness of the specialties, skills, and services of other helping personnel in the community.	17.5							

Competency	No.	Subcompetency	No.	1	2	3	4	5	NO	NE
	17.6	Acknowledge counselor misperceptions, mistakes, and limitations, as well as astute insights, successes, and potential.	17.6							
	17.7	Respond appropriately when personal concerns impair service to clients (seek counseling, consider temporarily discontinuing service to clients, and/or take other appropriate measures).	17.7							
18. Be committed to and uphold professional ethics.	18.1	Exhibit a thorough knowledge of ethical standards of professional organizations and credentialing bodies.	18.1							
	18.2	Examine personal ethics to resolve any conflicts with professional ethical standards.	18.2							
	18.3	Behave in accordance with professional ethical standards.	18.3							
	18.4	Educate coworkers, administrators, and clients regarding professional ethical standards of counselors.	18.4							
	18.5	Be familiar with and respect the ethical standards of coworkers representing professions other than counseling.	18.5							
				1 Low	2	3 Average	4	5 High	NO	NE

CHAPTER 2

COUNSELING COMPETENCIES FOR SELECTED ENVIRONMENTS AND POPULATIONS

2A. ADDICTION COUNSELING

GOAL STATEMENT: The professional counselor understands the etiology and dynamics of chemical dependence and other addictions, possesses the personality, characteristics, knowledge, and skills required of the effective helper, complies with ethical standards and, as appropriate to his or her credentials, educates the public concerning issues involved in recovery and growth and helps clients recover from addiction.

COMPETENCIES The counselor is a skilled professional who is able to:	**PERFORMANCE GUIDELINES** The professional counselor provides evidence of competence by demonstrating the ability to:		**ASSESSMENT**	Low 1	2	Average 3	4	High 5	NO	NE
1. Demonstrate an understanding of the disease concept and the etiology of chemical dependence and other addictive behaviors.	1.1	Recognize and explain the phases of the disease according to various models of addiction such as the Jellinek curve, the Johnson model, the Gitlow model, and others.	1.1							
	1.2	Describe the range of behaviors, from nonproblem behaviors to full addiction.	1.2							
	1.3	Explain the issues inherent in psychological dependence, including such issues as guilt, shame, and personal and social inadequacy.	1.3							
	1.4	Describe the pathological effect of mood-altering chemicals and behaviors on personality functioning.	1.4							

Competency		Skill		1	2	3	4	5	NO	NE
	1.5	Explain the role of denial in the disease process.	1.5							
	1.6	Describe and explain genetic factors, e.g., the nature-versus-nurture controversy over the etiology of dependence; identical twin studies.	1.6							
	1.7	Apply theories of etiology of dependence.	1.7							
	1.8	Specify the family's multigenerational role in the etiology of chemical abuse and addiction.	1.8							
2. Develop and maintain a working knowledge of pharmacology, toxicology, and the body's natural opiates (endorphins and enkephal-ins) as they relate to functions of the body.	2.1	Know the effects of moderate vs. heavy substance abuse or addiction behaviors on the central nervous system, peripheral nervous system, digestive system, cardiovascular system, pulmonary system, reproductive system, etc.	2.1							
	2.2	Stay current through continuing education.	2.2							
3. Classify the types of mood-altering chemicals frequently misused, i.e., sedative-hypnotics, barbiturates, stimulants, hallucinogens, cannabinoids, opiates, etc.	3.1	Recognize and specify the various pharmacological drugs that are misused and their emotional, physical, and psychological side effects.	3.1							
	3.2	Recognize and specify the various kinds of illegal drugs and their emotional, physical, and psychological effects.	3.2							
				1 Low	2	3 Average	4	5 High	NO	NE

COMPETENCIES The counselor is a skilled professional who is able to:	PERFORMANCE GUIDELINES The professional counselor provides evidence of competence by demonstrating the ability to:		ASSESSMENT	Low 1	2	Average 3	4	High 5	NO	NE
4. Demonstrate knowledge of the pharmaceutical treatment of mental disorders.	4.1	Specify the major categories of psychopharmaceuticals.	4.1							
	4.2	Specify the therapeutic intent of the major categories of psychopharmaceuticals.	4.2							
5. Demonstrate knowledge of how chemical dependence and other addictions affect family and other personal relationships.	5.1	Define family member roles established in response to a dependent family member; i.e., enabler, hero, scapegoat, lost child, mascot, addict's confidant, enabler's confidant, identified patient, surrogate spouse, etc.	5.1							
	5.2	Define the term "adult child of an alcoholic" (ACOA or ACA) and discuss symptoms common to many ACAs.	5.2							
	5.3	Define support groups available to family members of the chemically dependent or those with other addictions (e.g., food, gambling, sex, love).	5.3							
	5.4	Have a working knowledge of various counseling theories and methods used in family therapy.	5.4							
	5.5	Define the rationale, process, and techniques involved in marital and family therapy for the families of the chemically dependent or those with other addictions.	5.5							

Competency		Skill		1	2	3	4	5		NO	NE
6. Diagnose and assess chemical dependence and other addictions.	6.1	Recognize physical, behavioral, emotional, social, and spiritual symptoms of chemical dependence and other addiction(s).	6.1								
	6.2	Demonstrate familiarity with laboratory methods of screening, e.g., urinalysis, breath analysis, blood testing, etc.	6.2								
	6.3	Know the various screening instruments used to identify chemical dependence and other addictions; i.e., the DSM-III-R, Michigan Alcohol Screening Test (MAST), the 12 or 20 question lists, Adolescent Alcohol Involvement Scale, Problem Drinking Scale (PDS), Alcohol Use Inventory (AUI), the Comprehensive Drinker Profile (CDP), Cocaine Assessment, Minnesota Multiphasic Personality Inventory (MMPI), Macandrew Alcoholism Scale, etc.	6.3								
7. Demonstrate working knowledge of counseling and treatment methods, issues, and techniques commonly used in treating the chemically dependent and addicted.	7.1	Explain differences in the counseling process that result from chemical dependence or other addictions and their effects on the individual.	7.1								
	7.2	Specify how one's personal theory of counseling can be used to address issues of denial, lying, and dependence.	7.2								
				1 Low	2	3 Average	4	5 High		NO	NE

COMPETENCIES **The counselor is a skilled professional who is able to:**	PERFORMANCE GUIDELINES **The professional counselor provides evidence of competence by demonstrating the ability to:**		ASSESSMENT	Low 1	2	Average 3	4	High 5	NO	NE
(Continued) 7. Demonstrate working knowledge of counseling and treatment methods, issues, and techniques commonly used in treating the chemically dependent and addicted.	7.3	Specify the therapeutic group approaches available and their value in the treatment of the chemically dependent or those with other addictions.	7.3							
	7.4	Explain pharmacological methods of managing chemical abuse or other addictions; detoxification; and withdrawal.	7.4							
	7.5	Define the rationale for in-hospital treatment for the chemically dependent or those with other addictions.	7.5							
	7.6	Define the rationale for outpatient treatment for the chemically dependent or those with other addictions; after-care; and half-way houses.	7.6							
8. Be conversant with major issues involved in recovery and growth.	8.1	Explain the necessity of providing support systems to recovering individuals.	8.1							
	8.2	Specify the types of self-help groups available for specific kinds of addictions; e.g., Alcoholics Anonymous, Narcotics Anonymous, Codependents Anonymous, Al-Anon, Alateen, Sex and Love Addicts Anonymous, Gamblers Anonymous, and Overeaters Anonymous.	8.2							

Goal		Competency		1	2	3	4	5	NO	NE
	8.3	Demonstrate a working knowledge and understanding of the 12-step model of recovery.	8.3							
	8.4	Demonstrate techniques of intervention as applied to a substance abusive or addicted person.	8.4							
	8.5	Understand the problem of relapse and demonstrate methods and techniques that might be effective in lowering the probability of relapse.	8.5							
9. Develop a thorough knowledge of the relationship between addiction and suicide or addiction and violence.	9.1	Understand procedures for suicide intervention using models developed by suicidologists or various counseling theorists.	9.1							
	9.2	Understand problems of family violence, e.g., child sexual, emotional, and physical abuse and spouse battering, as they relate to substance abuse and other addictions.	9.2							
	9.3	Be fully familiar with community resources that deal with suicide and violence and continually update resource lists.	9.3							
10. Apply knowledge of ethical and legal issues and be familiar with community resources.	10.1	Know what constitutes an infraction of the law and the consequences of breaking the law; know what constitutes misdemeanor and felony.	10.1							

1 2 3 4 5
Low Average High

NO NE

COMPETENCIES **The counselor is a skilled professional who is able to:**	PERFORMANCE GUIDELINES **The professional counselor provides evidence of competence by demonstrating the ability to:**		ASSESSMENT	Low 1	2	Average 3	4	High 5	NO	NE
(Continued) 10. Apply knowledge of ethical and legal issues and be familiar with community resources.	10.2	Model ethical and legal behavior.	10.2							
	10.3	Obtain appropriate state and national credentials.	10.3							
	10.4	Be familiar with what law enforcement and other community agencies are doing in the areas of education and prevention.	10.4							
	10.5	Know what efforts are successful in reaching families, parents, and the addicts themselves with regard to alleviating the problem.	10.5							
	10.6	Conduct liaison with local, state, and national resource persons and organizations.	10.6							
	10.7	Join and participate in appropriate professional organizations.	10.7							

2B. CHILD AND ADOLESCENT COUNSELING

GOAL STATEMENT: The professional counselor for children and adolescents possesses the personality characteristics, knowledge, and basic demonstrated skills required of the effective helper, complies with ethical standards and, as appropriate to his or her credentials, demonstrates knowledge and skill in areas endemic to counseling with children and youth.

COMPETENCIES The counselor is a skilled professional who is able to:	**PERFORMANCE GUIDELINES** The professional counselor provides evidence of competence by demonstrating the ability to:		**ASSESSMENT**	Low 1	2	Average 3	4	High 5	NO	NE
1. Demonstrate conceptual knowledge of the unique characteristics of counseling with children by creating facilitative conditions.	1.1	Utilize developmentally appropriate counseling modalities and techniques including:	1.1							
	1.1a	Art therapy;	1.1a							
	1.1b	Bibliotherapy;	1.1b							
	1.1c	Game therapy;	1.1c							
	1.1d	Mutual storytelling; and	1.1d							
	1.1e	Play therapy.	1.1e							
	1.2	Demonstrate an understanding of the theoretical rationale for using:	1.2							
	1.2a	Art therapy;	1.2a							
	1.2b	Bibliotherapy;	1.2b							

COMPETENCIES The counselor is a skilled professional who is able to:	PERFORMANCE GUIDELINES The professional counselor provides evidence of competence by demonstrating the ability to:		ASSESSMENT	Low 1	2	Average 3	4	High 5	NO	NE
(Continued) 1. Demonstrate conceptual knowledge of the unique characteristics of counseling with children by creating facilitative conditions.	1.2c	Game therapy;	1.2c							
	1.2d	Mutual storytelling; and	1.2d							
	1.2e	Play therapy.	1.2e							
2. Demonstrate conceptual knowledge of the developmental counseling process with children.	2.1	Identify behavioral change in child clients.	2.1							
	2.2	Identify stages in the therapeutic process.	2.2							
	2.3	Assess inter- and intrapersonal points of reference indicating readiness for termination, including changes in play behavior.	2.3							
3. Demonstrate conceptual knowledge in dealing with difficult child relationship problems.	3.1	Calm the frightened child.	3.1							
	3.2	Establish contact with the resistant child.	3.2							
	3.3	Facilitate communication with the nonverbal child without requiring the child to verbalize (i.e., tracking behavior).	3.3							
	3.4	Establish therapeutic limits.	3.4							
4. Demonstrate conceptual knowledge of the technical and organizational aspects of counseling with children.	4.1	Select appropriate toys and materials for the chosen modality (e.g., art therapy, game therapy, play therapy).	4.1							

Competency		Skill		1	2	3	4	5	NO	NE
	4.2	Organize and structure the proper setting for the chosen modality.	4.2							
5. Demonstrate conceptual knowledge of the unique aspects of relating to parents when counseling with their children.	5.1	Explain the modalities of art therapy, bibliotherapy, game therapy, mutual storytelling, and play therapy to parents.	5.1							
	5.2	Deal effectively with parent resistance.	5.2							
	5.3	Protect the child's confidentiality appropriately.	5.3							
6. Help the adolescent resolve concerns of a particular stage of development.	6.1	Facilitate the exploration of sexuality.	6.1							
	6.2	Facilitate the initial establishment of independence and identity separate from parents and family.	6.2							
	6.3	Facilitate identity clarification and a beginning definition of life and career goals.	6.3							
7. Help the parents and family of the adolescent understand and accept the changes that arise during a particular stage of development.	7.1	Understand changes in family dynamics related to the adolescent stage of development.	7.1							
	7.2	Provide information and emotional support to the adolescent's parents and family to optimize functioning during adolescence.	7.2							
				1 Low	2	3 Average	4	5 High	NO	NE

COMPETENCIES The counselor is a skilled professional who is able to:	PERFORMANCE GUIDELINES The professional counselor provides evidence of competence by demonstrating the ability to:		ASSESSMENT	Low 1	2	Average 3	4	High 5	NO	NE
(Continued) 7. Help the parents and family of the adolescent understand and accept the changes that arise during a particular stage of development.	7.3	Provide consultation and training for parents to help them cope with situations particular to the adolescent stage of development.	7.3							
8. Demonstrate knowledge and understanding of issues and problems currently concerning adolescents.	8.1	Work with adolescents who are depressed and/or suicidal and their families.	8.1							
	8.2	Work with adolescents who are experiencing problems with drug and/or alcohol and their families.	8.2							
	8.3	Work with adjudicated adolescents and their families.	8.3							
	8.4	Work with pregnant adolescents and their families.	8.4							
	8.5	Work with adolescents who have eating disorders and their families.	8.5							
	8.6	Work with adolescents who are considering dropping out of school and their families.	8.6							
	8.7	Work with abused adolescents and their families.	8.7							

Competency		Skill		1 Low	2	3 Average	4	5 High	NO	NE
	8.8	Work with runaway adolescents and their families.	8.8							
9. Demonstrate knowledge and understanding of interpersonal strategies found to be effective with adolescents.	9.1	Use humor in a counseling relationship.	9.1							
	9.2	Be patient and flexible.	9.2							
	9.3	Explain the process of counseling and deal with client resistance and denial.	9.3							
	9.4	Be nonjudgmental.	9.4							
	9.5	Be concrete and immediate.	9.5							
10. Demonstrate knowledge and understanding of counseling techniques found to be effective with adolescents.	10.1	Conduct activity therapy sessions.	10.1							
	10.2	Use games therapeutically.	10.2							
	10.3	Capitalize on the growing importance of the peer group through counseling.	10.3							
	10.4	Teach problem solving and decision making.	10.4							

2C. COMMUNITY AND MENTAL HEALTH COUNSELING

GOAL STATEMENT: The professional counselor possesses the personality characteristics, knowledge, and skills required of the effective helper, complies with ethical standards and, as appropriate to his or her credentials, provides a full range of mental health services to the community.

COMPETENCIES The counselor is a skilled professional who is able to:	PERFORMANCE GUIDELINES The professional counselor provides evidence of competence by demonstrating the ability to:		ASSESSMENT	Low 1	2	Average 3	4	High 5	NO	NE
1. Demonstrate an understanding of the historical, philosophical, social, psychological, cultural, economic, and political implications of mental health counseling within the context of the mental health movement.	1.1	Understand the historical roots of worldwide and American mental health services.	1.1							
	1.2	Differentiate between the various philosophical approaches to mental health counseling.	1.2							
	1.3	Explain how social, psychological, and cultural differences apply to mental health counseling.	1.3							
	1.4	Understand the economic and political realities as they exist in the agency setting.	1.4							
2. Differentiate the unique professional identities of mental health counselors.	2.1	Explain the differences in competencies among and between the basic core providers of mental health counseling.	2.1							
	2.2	Advocate a team approach to service delivery using core providers.	2.2							

Goal		Objective		1	2	3	4	5	NO	NE
3. Understand structures and operations of professional organizations, credentialing mechanisms, training standards, and ethical and legal codes affecting mental health counselors.	3.1	Explain the differences between the various core-providing organizations.	3.1							
	3.2	Analyze differences between the various state licensing bodies and national and state credentialing bodies of core providers.	3.2							
	3.3	Interpret the differences between professional standards and legal statutes as they apply to core providers.	3.3							
4. Explain principles and demonstrate practices of research and evaluation as they relate to mental health counseling.	4.1	Differentiate the research and evaluation processes of mental health counseling from those for other forms of counseling.	4.1							
	4.2	Conduct research in the mental health field.	4.2							
5. Elaborate central issues of professional ethics, confidentiality, professional liability, privileged communication, client rights, and expert witness status.	5.1	Conduct staff development activities in the areas of:	5.1							
	5.1a	Ethical standards and issues;	5.1a							
	5.1b	Legal standards and issues;	5.1b							
	5.1b1	Privileged communication;	5.1b1							
	5.1b2	Professional liability; and	5.1b2							
	5.1b3	Expert witness requirements.	5.1b3							
				1 Low	2	3 Average	4	5 High	NO	NE

COMPETENCIES The counselor is a skilled professional who is able to:	PERFORMANCE GUIDELINES The professional counselor provides evidence of competence by demonstrating the ability to:		ASSESSMENT	Low 1	2	Average 3	4	High 5	NO	NE
(Continued) 5. Elaborate central issues of professional ethics, confidentiality, professional liability, privileged communication, client rights, and expert witness status.	5.2	Explore implications of the published codes of ethics of the various core service providing organizations.	5.2							
6. Demonstrate working knowledge of the administrative/business aspects of public and private mental health agencies.	6.1	Expedite personnel hiring and termination.	6.1							
	6.2	Expedite budget development.	6.2							
	6.3	Expedite personnel development and advancement.	6.3							
	6.4	Understand business purchasing and contracts.	6.4							
	6.5	Develop grant-writing capabilities.	6.5							
7. Deliniate the assumptions and roles of mental health counseling as a core provider discipline within the context of the health and human services system, including the historical, organizational, legal, and fiscal structures of public and private mental health care systems.	7.1	Implement professional communication contacts with other core providers.	7.1							
	7.2	Develop referral networks with other core providers.	7.2							
	7.3	Develop cooperative in-service training opportunities.	7.3							

Competency		Objective		1	2	3	4	5	NO	NE
8. Understand the place of mental health counseling within the confines of the medical model, in terms of both inpatient and outpatient care.	8.1	Establish and maintain positive working relationships with the medical community.	8.1							
	8.2	Educate the medical community regarding mental health counseling.	8.2							
9. Explain general principles and theories of community intervention, including inpatient, outpatient, partial treatment, and aftercare programs and facilities and the human services network available in the community.	9.1	Establish lines of communication within the human services network.	9.1							
	9.2	Develop interagency treatment plans when appropriate.	9.2							
10. Develop and implement appropriate prevention programs.	10.1	Explain general principles and theories of prevention programs within mental health counseling.	10.1							
	10.2	Develop and coordinate quality assurance and prevention programs.	10.2							
	10.3	Evaluate results of quality assurance and prevention programs.	10.3							
11. Apply theories and techniques of community needs assessment in order to design, implement, and evaluate mental health care programs and systems.	11.1	Carry out appropriate needs assessment programs.	11.1							
	11.2	Carry out follow-up of evaluation programs.	11.2							
				1 Low	2	3 Average	4	5 High	NO	NE

COMPETENCIES The counselor is a skilled professional who is able to:	PERFORMANCE GUIDELINES The professional counselor provides evidence of competence by demonstrating the ability to:		ASSESSMENT	Low 1	2	Average 3	4	High 5	NO	NE
12. Apply theories and principles of accountability and quality assurance programs.	12.1	Implement quality assurance programs as needed.	12.1							
	12.2	Evaluate quality assurance processes.	12.2							
13. Demonstrate working knowledge of the process of public and private grant proposal writing.	13.1	Write funding proposals as a way to supplement tax-based and other funding.	13.1							
	13.2	Collaborate in writing proposals with colleagues in other settings.	13.2							
14. Develop and implement cost-effective mental health programs.	14.1	Apply concepts of fiscal responsibility and cost containment in community agency finances.	14.1							
	14.2	Plan, develop, and implement cost-effective programs and services.	14.2							
	14.3	Coordinate interagency health counseling as a way to provide reasonably priced services.	14.3							
	14.4	Evaluate the cost-effectiveness of programs.	14.4							
15. Develop and implement appropriate diagnostic-based treatment programs.	15.1	Apply the principles and practices of etiology, diagnosis, and treatment of mental/emotional disorders and dysfunctional behaviors.	15.1							

Competency		Task		1 Low	2	3 Average	4	5 High	NO	NE
	15.2	Plan, develop, and implement a diagnostic-based program.	15.2							
	15.3	Coordinate interdisciplinary diagnostic and treatment programs.	15.3							
16. Demonstrate general principles of health promotion as applied to mental health.	16.1	Assess community need for health promotion as it applies to mental health.	16.1							
	16.2	Implement appropriate mental health promotion programs.	16.2							
	16.3	Evaluate mental health promotion programs.	16.3							
17. Plan, develop, and coordinate interdisciplinary efforts in clinical and test-based assessment endeavors.	17.1	Apply theories, models, and methods of assessment of mental status and identification of psychopathological behavior.	17.1							
	17.2	Conduct assessments and interpret results.	17.2							
	17.3	Utilize appropriate methods of evaluation.	17.3							
18. Explain and demonstrate uses of the current *Diagnostic and Statistical Manual of Mental Disorders* (DSM-III-R) of the American Psychiatric Association.	18.1	Coordinate the use of the current DSM-III-R among the core service providers.	18.1							
	18.2	Educate all staff as to the proper use of the DSM-III-R.	18.2							

COMPETENCIES The counselor is a skilled professional who is able to:	PERFORMANCE GUIDELINES The professional counselor provides evidence of competence by demonstrating the ability to:		ASSESSMENT							
				Low 1	2	Average 3	4	High 5	NO	NE
19. Develop, plan, and coordinate an appropriate client appraisal service.	19.1	Conduct a variety of appraisal techniques including clinical assessment, projective and nonprojective techniques, achievement tests, aptitude and intelligence tests, interest inventories, values and temperament surveys and related instruments, and intrepret the results.	19.1							
	19.2	Educate all staff as to appropriate uses of assessment instruments.	19.2							
	19.3	Interpret the results of assessment instruments within a meaningful context.	19.3							
20. Encourage appropriate use of psychotherapy that is designed to meet the special needs of clients.	20.1	Explain the various theories of psychotherapy as they apply to initiating, maintaining, coordinating, and terminating therapy with mentally and emotionally impaired clients.	20.1							
	20.2	Educate various core providers as to the use of multimodal counseling approaches.	20.2							
21. Coordinate the use of diagnostic data in the assessment process.	21.1	Incorporate and use social histories and psychiatric diagnostic data in the assessment, intervention, and prevention processes.	21.1							

Competency		Skill		1 Low	2	3 Average	4	5 High	NO	NE
	21.2	Coordinate ongoing assessment in order to monitor client change.	21.2							
22. Implement appropriate strategies with appropriate clients.	22.1	Demonstrate a working knowledge of the process of therapy as it applies to crisis intervention, and brief, intermediate, and long-term intervention strategies.	22.1							
	22.2	Modify intervention strategies as client needs change over time.	22.2							
23. Apply psychopharmacological information in contacts with clients within a meaningful context.	23.1	Explain the basic classifications, indications, and contraindications of the commonly prescribed psychopharmacological medications.	23.1							
	23.2	Utilize a team-treatment approach with psychiatrists and psychiatric nurses.	23.2							
	23.3	Understand the basic effects and side effects of psychopharmacological medications.	23.3							
	23.4	Monitor medication use with all clients.	23.4							
	23.5	Maintain regular consultation with psychiatrists.	23.5							
24. Apply differential assessment/ management techniques.	24.1	Understand the process involved in and conduct intake and initial interviews with mental health clients for the purpose of assessment and case assignment/ management.	24.1							

COMPETENCIES The counselor is a skilled professional who is able to:	PERFORMANCE GUIDELINES The professional counselor provides evidence of competence by demonstrating the ability to:		ASSESSMENT							
				Low 1	2	Average 3	4	High 5	NO	NE
(Continued) 24. Apply differential assessment/ management techniques.	24.2	Coordinate assessment/management approaches among the core providers.	24.2							
25. Model professional career development.	25.1	Maintain active membership in appropri-ate professional organizations.	25.1							
	25.2	Obtain appropriate state and national professional credentials.	25.2							
	25.3	Develop and implement appropriate internal training programs.	25.3							
	25.4	Evaluate training outcomes.	25.4							
	25.5	Participate in and support staff participa-tion in external training programs and continuing education activities.	25.5							

2D. GROUP COUNSELING

GOAL STATEMENT: The professional counselor possesses the personality characteristics, knowledge, and skills required of the effective helper; complies with ethical standards; as appropriate to his or her credentials, is able to discern when individual or group counseling would be most helpful; understands basic principles of group dynamics; and is familiar with major group theories, stages of group development, group member roles, and research related to group counseling.

COMPETENCIES **The counselor is a skilled professional who is able to:**	PERFORMANCE GUIDELINES **The professional counselor provides evidence of competence by demonstrating the ability to:**		ASSESSMENT	Low 1	2	Average 3	4	High 5	NO	NE
1. Discern when individual or group counseling would be most helpful for the problem presented and for the client. (This implies recognition of referral responsibility when appropriate.)	1.1	Specify the types of problems that are particularly suited to group or individual counseling.	1.1							
	1.2	Structure specialized groups as to topic and purpose as well as membership.	1.2							
	1.3	Specify the effectiveness of both peer and traditional models on individual behavior.	1.3							
	1.4	Coordinate and sequence a client's participation in both individual and group counseling sessions.	1.4							
	1.5	Explain how the power of groups can be both advantageous and disadvantageous to members.	1.5							

COMPETENCIES The counselor is a skilled professional who is able to:	PERFORMANCE GUIDELINES The professional counselor provides evidence of competence by demonstrating the ability to:		ASSESSMENT	Low 1	2	Average 3	High 4	5	NO	NE
2. Use principles of group dynamics and group therapeutic conditions in various group activities that facilitate attitude and behavior change appropriate to the age level of the client.	2.1	Display a working knowledge of group dynamics such as:	2.1							
	2.1a	Content and process variables;	2.1a							
	2.1b	Various leadership styles; and	2.1b							
	2.1c	The conditions under which groups promote healthy growth.	2.1c							
	2.2	Display a working knowledge of developmental tasks and coping behaviors of different age levels and the skill to use various group techniques appropriate for client level including:	2.2							
	2.2a	Play and activity groups;	2.2a							
	2.2b	Modeling-social learning techniques; and	2.2b							
	2.2c	Role playing and psychodrama.	2.2c							
	2.3	Observe and record verbal and nonverbal interaction in groups, following predetermined cues and procedures for making such observations.	2.3							

Competency	No.	Skill	No.	1 Low	2	3 Average	4	5 High	NO	NE
	2.3a	Use the anecdotal method of observation and recording to report the significant components of individual and group interaction.	2.3a							
	2.3b	Chart group interaction through the use of an appropriate interaction tool.	2.3b							
	2.3c	Rate the initiative and responsive dimensions of group interaction.	2.3c							
	2.3d	Record the operant level and chart baseline data on selected behaviors as they emerge in the group (e.g., various physical phenomena, hostile statements, etc.).	2.3d							
3. Demonstrate a familiarity with the unique characteristics of at least three of the major group theories and the persons associated with their development.	3.1	Communicate and use appropriate and consistent methodologies included in at least three of the following group theories:	3.1							
	3.1a	Adlerian psychology;	3.1a							
	3.1b	Behavioral group counseling;	3.1b							
	3.1c	Developmental group counseling;	3.1c							
	3.1d	Gestalt group therapy;	3.1d							
	3.1e	Group psychodrama;	3.1e							
	3.1f	Human resource development training;	3.1f							

COMPETENCIES The counselor is a skilled professional who is able to:	PERFORMANCE GUIDELINES The professional counselor provides evidence of competence by demonstrating the ability to:		ASSESSMENT	Low 1	2	Average 3	4	High 5	NO	NE
(Continued) 3. Demonstrate a familiarity with the unique characteristics of at least three of the major group theories and the persons associated with their development.	3.1g	Person-centered group therapy;	3.1g							
	3.1h	Rational-emotive therapy;	3.1h							
	3.1i	Reality therapy;	3.1i							
	3.1j	Transactional analysis;	3.1j							
	3.1k	Family therapy groups; and	3.1k							
	3.1l	Addiction or recovery groups.	3.1l							
4. Demonstrate a familiarity with the history of group work and the important individuals/organizations who have contributed to its growth, such as:	4.1a	J.H. Pratt;	4.1a							
	4.1b	Alfred Adler;	4.1b							
	4.1c	J.L. Moreno;	4.1c							
	4.1d	S.R. Slavson;	4.1d							
	4.1e	C.R. Rogers;	4.1e							
	4.1f	National Training Laboratory;	4.1f							
	4.1g	The Human Potential Movement;	4.1g							
	4.1h	Fritz Perls;	4.1h							
	4.1i	Merle M. Ohlsen;	4.1i							

				1 Low	2	3 Average	4	5 High	NO	NE
	4.1j	C.G. Kemp;	4.1j							
	4.1k	G.M. Gazda; and	4.1k							
	4.1l	I.D. Yalom.	4.1l							
5. Demonstrate competence in dealing with terms specific to group counseling by discriminating among the various kinds of group activities.	5.1	Adequately define and explain the differences in orientation, methodology, procedures, leadership qualifications, and client population associated with:	5.1							
	5.1a	Group guidance;	5.1a							
	5.1b	Group counseling;	5.1b							
	5.1c	Group psychotherapy; and	5.1c							
	5.1d	Human relations training.	5.1d							
	5.2	Display a functional knowledge of the following terms and concepts and their application to groups:	5.2							
	5.2a	Group dynamics;	5.2a							
	5.2b	T-groups;	5.2b							
	5.2c	Psychodrama;	5.2c							
	5.2d	Open and closed groups;	5.2d							
	5.2e	Self-help and support groups;	5.2e							

COMPETENCIES The counselor is a skilled professional who is able to:	PERFORMANCE GUIDELINES The professional counselor provides evidence of competence by demonstrating the ability to:		ASSESSMENT	Low 1	2	Average 3	4	High 5	NO	NE
(Continued) 5. Demonstrate competence in dealing with terms specific to group counseling by discriminating among the various kinds of group activities.	5.2f	Specific issue groups;	5.2f							
	5.2g	Procedural rules for groups; and	5.2g							
	5.2h	Process analysis.	5.2h							
6. Communicate familiarity with a number of group growth and intervention systems and advise as to the appropriate group activity.	6.1	Function as a member or leader in the following kinds of group experiences:	6.1							
	6.1a	An encounter group;	6.1a							
	6.1b	A family therapy group; and	6.1b							
	6.1c	A play-therapy or an activity- therapy group.	6.1c							
	6.2	Colead ongoing group sessions in conjunction with an instructor, supervisor, or selected colleague.	6.2							
	6.3	Describe and/or experience various specialized methods and techniques in group counseling such as:	6.3							
	6.3a	Critique of group tapes by self or others;	6.3a							
	6.3b	Focused feedback;	6.3b							

Competency		Item		1	2	3	4	5	NO	NE
	6.3c	Observation of group counseling (live or taped);	6.3c							
	6.3d	Systematic desensitization;	6.3d							
	6.3e	Psychodrama;	6.3e							
	6.3f	Modeling;	6.3f							
	6.3g	Role playing;	6.3g							
	6.3h	Extended sessions or marathon groups; and	6.3h							
	6.3i	Issue groups specific to the counselor's expertise such as stress management groups, assertiveness groups, and team-building groups.	6.3i							
7. Demonstrate a familiarity with the typical stages of group development and appropriate intervention strategies and leader behaviors.	7.1	Organize and prepare for a group and get the initial group started.	7.1							
	7.2	Explain the beginning stages of a group.	7.2							
	7.3	Explain the working stages.	7.3							
	7.4	Explain the ending stages and termination procedures.	7.4							

1 2 3 4 5 — Low Average High   NO NE

COMPETENCIES The counselor is a skilled professional who is able to:	PERFORMANCE GUIDELINES The professional counselor provides evidence of competence by demonstrating the ability to:		ASSESSMENT	Low 1	2	Average 3	4	High 5	NO	NE
8. Indicate an awareness of the most frequently observed facilitative and debilitative roles that group members may take, along with relevant management strategies.	8.1	Describe and work with:	8.1							
	8.1a	The compulsive talker or monopolizing member;	8.1a							
	8.1b	The silent member;	8.1b							
	8.1c	The group clown;	8.1c							
	8.1d	The intellectualizer;	8.1d							
	8.1e	The rescuer;	8.1e							
	8.1f	The attacker;	8.1f							
	8.1g	The alienated member;	8.1g							
	8.1h	The withdrawn member;	8.1h							
	8.1i	The overly dependent member; and	8.1i							
	8.1j	The member who gives inappropriate advice.	8.1j							
9. Be conversant with the body of research related to group counseling, both landmark and current, particularly as it relates to one's area of specialty.	9.1	Stay current with professional literature in areas such as:	9.1							
	9.1a	School counseling;	9.1a							

				1	2	3	4	5	NO	NE
	9.1b	Student development work;	9.1b							
	9.1c	Community agencies;	9.1c							
	9.1d	Mental health facilities; and	9.1d							
	9.1e	Specific issue groups such as groups for depression, AIDS, eating disorders, the elderly, women, chronic diseases, and chemical abuse and other addictions.	9.1e							
10. Demonstrate personal behaviors and a sensitivity to issues that indicate an appreciation of ethical practices in group work.	10.1	Relate critically to specific professional guidelines that address ethics in group work, such as:	10.1							
	10.1a	Providing information and orienting new group members;	10.1a							
	10.1b	Screening potential group members;	10.1b							
	10.1c	Maintaining confidentiality;	10.1c							
	10.1d	Working with voluntary or involuntary participants;	10.1d							
	10.1e	Procedures for leaving the group;	10.1e							
	10.1f	Protecting group members against undue coercion and pressure, intimidation, and physical threats;	10.1f							
				Low		Average		High		

COMPETENCIES **The counselor is a skilled professional who is able to:**		PERFORMANCE GUIDELINES **The professional counselor provides evidence of competence by demonstrating the ability to:**	ASSESSMENT	Low 1	2	Average 3	4	High 5	NO	NE
(Continued) 10. Demonstrate personal behaviors and a sensitivity to issues that indicate an appreciation of ethical practices in group work.	10.1g	Imposing counselor values on group members;	10.1g							
	10.1h	Treating each group member equitably and equally;	10.1h							
	10.1i	Avoiding dual relationships;	10.1i							
	10.1j	Using group techniques in which the leader is not trained;	10.1j							
	10.1k	Consulting with members and other professionals between group meetings;	10.1k							
	10.1l	Terminating the group;	10.1l							
	10.1m	Conducting evaluation and follow-up procedures;	10.1m							
	10.1n	Managing referral to other appropriate professionals; and	10.1n							
	10.1o	Continuing the leader's professional development.	10.1o							

2E. HIGHER EDUCATION COUNSELING

GOAL STATEMENT: The professional counselor possesses the personality characteristics, knowledge, and skills required of the effective helper, complies with ethical standards and, as appropriate to his or her credentials, develops and maintains effective counseling, consultation, and supervision skills in serving all members of his or her higher education community.

COMPETENCIES **The counselor is a skilled professional who is able to:**	PERFORMANCE GUIDELINES **The professional counselor provides evidence of competence by demonstrating the ability to:**		ASSESSMENT	Low 1	2	Average 3	4	High 5	NO	NE
1. Be cognizant of the historical, current, and future trends and philosophies of college and university student services with an emphasis on counseling centers' function in institutions of higher education.	1.1	Identify major historical events, fundamental ideas and philosophies, and relevant theories that have shaped policies in college and university student services with a specific focus on personal adjustment and career counseling.	1.1							
	1.2	Articulate basic issues encompassing professional and ethical standards that arise in the formulation and implementation of student development services in higher education.	1.2							
	1.3	Possess a working knowledge of the current American Association for Counseling and Development's *Ethical Standards* and the American College Personnel Association's *Statement of Ethical Principles and Standards.*	1.3							

COMPETENCIES **The counselor is a skilled professional who is able to:**	PERFORMANCE GUIDELINES **The professional counselor provides evidence of competence by demonstrating the ability to:**		ASSESSMENT	Low 1	2	Average 3	4	High 5	NO	NE
2. Make an accurate assessment of the characteristics, attitudes, and behaviors of university and college students (emphasizing minorities and nontraditional students) and respond to their personal, social, and educational needs with preventive, developmental, and/or remedial services.	2.1	Survey students' needs for personal and career counseling.	2.1							
	2.2	Employ needs analyses and environmental assessment techniques in identifying and understanding the types of services required to enhance students' development.	2.2							
	2.3	Apply methods of survey research in the study of significant social and educational concerns of college and university students.	2.3							
	2.4	Monitor the impact of the campus atmosphere on specific populations such as minority students, returning adults, and the disabled.	2.4							
	2.5	Design and implement career and personal counseling services for students to promote their mental health and academic development.	2.5							
	2.6	Respect individual differences within subgroups based on economic, ethnic, and social status in relation to educational and personal growth and development.	2.6							

Competency		Performance Indicator		1 Low	2	3 Average	4	5 High	NO	NE
3. Distinguish among the theories, models, and processes of: consultation, organizational development, decision making, and conflict resolution, and implement their application in working with college and university populations.	3.1	Exhibit knowledge of consultation models: dyadic, triadic, process, and organizational development; consult and facilitate transactions with the mediator or consultee.	3.1							
	3.2	Delineate the consultant's/consultee's roles and responsibilities, identify the client and client rights, define pertinent problem areas, and intervene judiciously in achieving designated goals.	3.2							
	3.3	Effectively engage in the procedural steps of the consultation process: Gain entry; appraise the environment; make a diagnosis; collect data; establish a collaborative relationship; develop resources; facilitate decision making; and terminate upon completion of goals.	3.3							
	3.4	Provide skillful services as a mental health consultant to college and university students, faculty, administrators, and the university community.	3.4							
	3.5	Use concepts from decision-making and conflict-resolution theories in developing problem-solving strategies within a college and university environment.	3.5							
	3.6	Draw upon theories of group dynamics, interactions, and processes in making interventions with campuswide groups.	3.6							

COMPETENCIES The counselor is a skilled professional who is able to:	PERFORMANCE GUIDELINES The professional counselor provides evidence of competence by demonstrating the ability to:		ASSESSMENT	Low 1	2	Average 3	4	High 5	NO	NE
3. (Continued)	3.7	Apply professional and ethical standards in working with college and university organizations and facilitate their implementation.	3.7							
4. Interpret and apply research methodologies, designs, and statistical analyses in the evaluation of college and university counseling centers' services.	4.1	Write proposals and grants.	4.1							
	4.2	Demonstrate an understanding of principles of experimental design and types of research methodologies.	4.2							
	4.3	Distinguish among the kinds of statistical analyses used in interpreting data.	4.3							
	4.4	Plan, conduct, and interpret program evaluations of campuswide student services.	4.4							
5. Exhibit a knowledge of conceptions and theories about developmental phases of the life cycle and recognize the ecological context within which psychosocial and cultural factors influence human growth and development.	5.1	Apply cognitive and psychosocial developmental theories (such as those posited by Perry's model of intellectual and ethical development; Chickering's theory of student development; Kohlberg's and Erikson's developmental theories; and Piaget's concepts of maturation of cognitive structuring) in helping students cope effectively with developmental tasks and transitions.	5.1							

Competency	No.	Objective	No.	1	2	3	4	5	NO	NE
	5.2	Address concepts of deviance applied to young adults in the context of normal development and mental wellness.	5.2							
	5.3	Draw upon the person-environment interaction model and related campus ecosystem designs in making appropriate interventions to promote student involvement, influence, and development.	5.3							
	5.4	Identify special populations (minority and nontraditional students such as returning adult learners, gay and lesbian students, international students, and disabled students) in need of student development services and promote the use of these services.	5.4							
6. Display a functional knowledge of both personal counseling and career development theories and related research, and implement behavioral factors that contribute to clients' change as a result of the counseling relationship.	6.1	Enhance the overall mental and physical development of student athletes by implementing personal and career counseling services.	6.1							
	6.2	Assist in establishing AIDS-related policies and counseling and referral procedures in working with a college and university population.	6.2							
				Low		Average		High		

COMPETENCIES The counselor is a skilled professional who is able to:	PERFORMANCE GUIDELINES The professional counselor provides evidence of competence by demonstrating the ability to:		ASSESSMENT	Low 1	2	Average 3	High 4	5	NO	NE
(Continued) 6. Display a functional knowledge of both personal counseling and career development theories and related research, and implement behavioral factors that contribute to clients' change as a result of the counseling relationship.	6.3	Demonstrate a sensitivity to and knowledge of issues and problems frequently encountered by special populations (minority and nontraditional students such as returning adult learners, gay and lesbian students, international students, and disabled students) and make appropriate interventions.	6.3							
	6.4	Address the practical issues, including ethical and counseling concerns, in the diagnosis, treatment, and prevention of alcohol and drug-related problems on campus.	6.4							
	6.5	Act as a consultant and educator in disseminating information about substance abuse on campus including: consumption patterns, remission, relapse, counseling referrals, and prevention strategies.	6.5							
	6.6	Advocate and promote drug-free environments on college and university campuses.	6.6							
	6.7	Identify students with lethal risk and recognize the variables that contribute to acts of suicide.	6.7							

				1	2	3	4	5	NO	NE
	6.8	Skillfully make assessments, interventions, and appropriate referrals for students in crisis.	6.8							
	6.9	Develop a referral mechanism with community agencies and student service offices.	6.9							
	6.10	Demonstrate a sensitivity to and familiarity with issues, interventions, and prevention strategies in dealing with sexual aggression, harassment, and coercion on campus.	6.10							
	6.11	Be aware of the variables and make interventions that will positively influence college and university student performance and retention.	6.11							
	6.12	Develop retention strategies geared to high-risk students such as transfer students, incoming freshmen, minorities, and returning adult students.	6.12							
	6.13	Develop programs and services to help disabled students overcome physical and psychological barriers to their personal growth and development.	6.13							
	6.14	Assist students in appraising their skills, attitudes, and achievements as they develop strategies for educational and career advancement.	6.14							
				Low		Average		High		

COMPETENCIES The counselor is a skilled professional who is able to:		PERFORMANCE GUIDELINES The professional counselor provides evidence of competence by demonstrating the ability to:	ASSESSMENT	Low 1	2	Average 3	4	High 5	NO	NE
(Continued) 6. Display a functional knowledge of both personal counseling and career development theories and related research, and implement behavioral factors that contribute to clients' change as a result of the counseling relationship.	6.15	Apply theories of career counseling and development in working with students making decisions about their education and career development.	6.15							
	6.16	Demonstrate a knowledge of concepts, theories, and applications for recommending students to either time-limited or long-term counseling.	6.16							
	6.17	Contact campuswide organizations and offer outreach programs that address the personal, career, and educational needs of students.	6.17							
7. Understand legal and ethical aspects of student development services in higher education, personnel supervision and evaluation, unionization and collective bargaining, budget and finance, governance and policy-making, human resource development, and information management.	7.1	Display a knowledge of students' legal rights and institutional ethical responsibilities as related to due process, search and seizure, and factors regarding disciplinary matters.	7.1							
	7.2	Demonstrate a familiarity with the conceptions, issues, and problems of fundamental management and human relations principles inherent in institutions of higher education by establishing an effective organizational culture and identity.	7.2							

Competency		Indicator		1 Low	2	3 Average	4	5 High	NO	NE
	7.3	Conduct periodic audits of human resource management practices.	7.3							
	7.4	Contribute to developing evaluation and accountability systems within various organizational facets of higher education.	7.4							
8. Understand principles of human resource training.	8.1	Consult with organizations regarding the development of training programs for student helpers such as residence hall advisors and paraprofessionals.	8.1							
	8.2	Evaluate the outcomes of specific training programs.	8.2							
	8.3	Assist professionals and paraprofessionals in developing knowledge and skills in the delivery of personal and career counseling services.	8.3							
9. Develop and coordinate programs and maintain liaison contacts with faculty, staff, and administrators.	9.1	Develop a cooperative relationship with other college and university staff, faculty, and administrators to gain their active support in the delivery of personal and career counseling services.	9.1							
	9.2	Coordinate and refine programs.	9.2							

COMPETENCIES The counselor is a skilled professional who is able to:	PERFORMANCE GUIDELINES The professional counselor provides evidence of competence by demonstrating the ability to:		ASSESSMENT	Low 1	2	Average 3	4	High 5	NO	NE
10. Provide training and supervision of advanced graduate students, interns, and paraprofessionals in the development of professional skills.	10.1	Select, train, and develop therapeutic competence in supervisees.	10.1							
	10.2	Utilize the theoretical models, techniques, and approaches to effective training and supervision.	10.2							

2F. INDIVIDUAL COUNSELING

GOAL STATEMENT: The professional counselor develops, maintains, and provides effective counseling skills that help clients grow toward personal goals and strengthen their capacity to cope with life situations.

COMPETENCIES **The counselor is a skilled professional who is able to:**	PERFORMANCE GUIDELINES **The professional counselor provides evidence of competence by demonstrating the ability to:**		ASSESSMENT							
				Low 1	2	Average 3	4	High 5	NO	NE
1. Demonstrate an understanding of the basic principles of human growth and development and how they affect the counseling process.	1.1	Describe the fundamental principles of individual development (physical, cognitive, emotional, moral, social, and spiritual) through the life span.	1.1							
	1.2	Explain the family life cycle and its effects on individual behavior.	1.2							
	1.3	Assess clients' developmental levels and developmental issues.	1.3							
	1.4	Communicate effectively with clients of different ages and developmental levels.	1.4							
2. Understand and explain how cultural variations affect the counseling process.	2.1	Explain the value, mores, and behavioral patterns associated with various cultural or subcultural groups represented by both the counselor and individual clients.	2.1							
	2.2	Cite basic physical and psychological needs and cultural universals that constitute a basis for commonality between all humans.	2.2							

COMPETENCIES The counselor is a skilled professional who is able to:	PERFORMANCE GUIDELINES The professional counselor provides evidence of competence by demonstrating the ability to:		ASSESSMENT	Low 1	2	Average 3	4	High 5	NO	NE
(Continued) 2. Understand and explain how cultural variations affect the counseling process.	2.3	Assess the extent to which membership in or affiliation with a particular culture or subculture affects the values and behavior of both the counselor and individual clients.	2.3							
	2.4	Increase awareness of personal prejudices regarding racism, sexism, ageism, and/or poverty, and attempt to relinquish such prejudices.	2.4							
	2.5	Develop counseling techniques to bridge cultural differences that may exist between counselor and client.	2.5							
3. Explain the major counseling theories and their associated procedures and techniques.	3.1	For each major counseling theory (e.g., Adlerian, behavioral, cognitive, Gestalt, person-centered, transactional analysis), explain the following in the vocabulary associated with that theory:	3.1							
	3.1a	Philosophical assumptions;	3.1a							
	3.1b	View of human nature, including innate drives and tendencies for all humans;	3.1b							
	3.1c	Personality development and structure;	3.1c							
	3.1d	Etiology of maladaptive behavior;	3.1d							

Competency		Objective		1	2	3	4	5	NO	NE
	3.1e	Assessment of clients;	3.1e							
	3.1f	Necessary and sufficient conditions under which psychological growth and/or behavioral change can or will occur;	3.1f							
	3.1g	Specific procedures and techniques that facilitate constructive client change; and	3.1g							
	3.1h	Rationale for differential treatment based on a client's developmental level, cultural affiliation, or problem(s).	3.1h							
	3.2	Identify commonalities and differences among the major counseling theories.	3.2							
	3.3	Specify limitations of each major counseling theory.	3.3							
	3.4	Explain how each major theory would conceptualize and treat a given case example.	3.4							
4. Develop a personal approach to counseling that is consistent with the counselor's values and beliefs.	4.1	Specify the philosophical assumptions, as well as beliefs about human nature, personality development, etiology of maladaptive behavior, and conditions for change to which the counselor ascribes; identify as the counselor's guiding theory the major theory with which the counselor's beliefs most closely align.	4.1							

1 2 3 4 5 NO NE
Low Average High

COMPETENCIES The counselor is a skilled professional who is able to:	PERFORMANCE GUIDELINES The professional counselor provides evidence of competence by demonstrating the ability to:		ASSESSMENT	Low 1	2	Average 3	4	High 5	NO	NE
(Continued) 4. Develop a personal approach to counseling that is consistent with the counselor's values and beliefs.	4.2	Describe and enact the counselor's role and responsibilities as specified by the guiding theory.	4.2							
	4.3	Describe and enact the procedures and techniques specified by or consistent with the guiding theory.	4.3							
	4.4	Describe and identify the stages of the counseling process delineated by the guiding theory.	4.4							
	4.5	Apply the guiding theory to describe the client's therapeutic goals, and identify client movement toward and achievement of those goals.	4.5							
5. Establish and maintain a constructive, facilitative, and ongoing relationship with clients.	5.1	Communicate genuine warmth by expressing an attitude of nonpossessive caring for the client and the client's welfare.	5.1							
	5.2	Communicate genuine respect for the client's inherent worth by discriminating between the client as a person and specific client behaviors that may be maladaptive.	5.2							
	5.3	Communicate genuine respect for the client's freedom of choice and belief in the client's capacity for responsible choice.	5.3							

Objective	No.	Competency	No.	1	2	3	4	5	NO	NE
	5.4	Communicate genuine empathy by being able to see the client's world from the client's point of view.	5.4							
	5.5	Communicate nonjudgmental openness and receptivity to ideas and behaviors similar to or different from those valued by the counselor.	5.5							
	5.6	Communicate hope by expressing belief in the client's potential.	5.6							
6. Demonstrate basic counseling skills used in most or all of the major counseling theories.	6.1	Use appropriate attending behavior.	6.1							
	6.2	Use brief verbal and nonverbal responses that constitute minimal encouragement for the client to continue.	6.2							
	6.3	Adapt terminology to the language level of the client.	6.3							
	6.4	Paraphrase content of client messages.	6.4							
	6.5	Reflect feelings expressed verbally or nonverbally by clients.	6.5							
	6.6	Ask open-ended questions when possible and closed-ended questions when necessary.	6.6							
	6.7	Communicate in specific and concrete, rather than general and abstract, terms.	6.7							
				1 Low	2	3 Average	4	5 High	NO	NE

COMPETENCIES The counselor is a skilled professional who is able to:	PERFORMANCE GUIDELINES The professional counselor provides evidence of competence by demonstrating the ability to:		ASSESSMENT	Low 1	2	Average 3	4	High 5	NO	NE
(Continued) 6. Demonstrate basic counseling skills used in most or all of the major counseling theories.	6.8	Confront discrepancies in client communication.	6.8							
	6.9	Reframe client communications.	6.9							
	6.10	Use interpretation skills appropriate to the counselor's guiding theory, such as formulating and communicating competing hypotheses to explain the client's situation and experiences.	6.10							
	6.11	Disclose ideas, feelings, and experiences in a relevant, timely, and open manner.	6.11							
7. Conduct an intake interview at the beginning of the counseling relationship life cycle.	7.1	Address clients' potential or expressed attitudes of apprehension, reluctance, or hostility toward the counseling process.	7.1							
	7.2	Communicate to the client that the counseling relationship is one of mutual consent; that the client is free to continue or terminate the relationship; and that the counselor is free to make a professional referral when it is deemed to be in the client's best interest.	7.2							
	7.3	Specify the scope and limitations of confidentiality and demonstrate the ability to communicate this information to clients.	7.3							

Competency	No.	Skill	No.	1	2	3	4	5		NO	NE
	7.4	Explain to each client the nature of the counseling relationship and the conditions the client should expect.	7.4								
	7.5	Develop and provide each client with a disclosure statement covering the nature of the practice, limits of confidentiality, and conditions of referral.	7.5								
	7.6	Develop a written and/or verbal contract specifying mutually agreed upon therapeutic goals.	7.6								
8. Conduct counseling sessions in the working stage(s) of the counseling relationship life cycle.	8.1	Specify and demonstrate various procedures for opening counseling sessions.	8.1								
	8.2	Foster a sense of continuity throughout a series of counseling sessions.	8.2								
	8.3	Facilitate and periodically assess client movement toward therapeutic goals.	8.3								
	8.4	Reassess and reformulate therapeutic goals in light of new information and developments.	8.4								
	8.5	Specify and demonstrate various procedures for closing counseling sessions.	8.5								
				1 Low	**2**	**3 Average**	**4**	**5 High**		**NO**	**NE**

COMPETENCIES The counselor is a skilled professional who is able to:	PERFORMANCE GUIDELINES The professional counselor provides evidence of competence by demonstrating the ability to:		ASSESSMENT	Low 1	2	Average 3	4	High 5	NO	NE
9. Manage the termination phase of the counseling relationship life cycle.	9.1	Acknowledge when clients are approaching achievement of therapeutic goals.	9.1							
	9.2	Address separation issues in a manner appropriate for each client.	9.2							
	9.3	Specify conditions for follow-up, when appropriate.	9.3							
10. Assess clients appropriately.	10.1	Explain appropriate procedures for the administration and interpretation of widely used standardized and nonstandardized methods of assessment.	10.1							
	10.2	Utilize methods of assessment that are consistent with the counselor's guiding theory and the client's therapeutic welfare.	10.2							
	10.3	Utilize standardized diagnostic nomenclature such as the DSM-III-R.	10.3							
	10.4	Discriminate carefully among the data gathered about a client to make specific diagnostic determinations, including the four axes of the DSM-III-R.	10.4							
11. Discern the counseling mode most facilitative to the concerns presented by the client.	11.1	Consistent with the counselor's guiding theory, adapt the counseling process to the unique characteristics and needs of the client.	11.1							

				1	2	3	4	5	NO	NE
	11.2	Consistent with the counselor's guiding theory and with the client's consent, enter the client's natural environment and/or enlist others in the client's environment to assist in carrying out specific remedial or preventive programs for the client.	11.2							
	11.3	Specify the types of problems especially amenable to individual, group, or family counseling.	11.3							
	11.4	Coordinate and sequence an individual client's concurrent participation in family or group counseling.	11.4							
12. Recognize and respond appropriately to personal and professional limitations.	12.1	Recognize when personal, ethical, or legal limitations of individual counseling have been or may have been exceeded.	12.1							
	12.2	Seek case consultation only with other appropriate professional personnel; discriminate carefully among client data to determine which data can be appropriately shared in consultation.	12.2							
	12.3	Seek to enhance counseling skills through continuing education such as periodic supervision by other qualified professionals, attendance at professional development seminars, and familiarity with the current counseling literature.	12.3							
				Low		Average		High		

COMPETENCIES The counselor is a skilled professional who is able to:	PERFORMANCE GUIDELINES The professional counselor provides evidence of competence by demonstrating the ability to:		ASSESSMENT	Low 1	2	Average 3	4	High 5	NO	NE
(Continued) 12. Recognize and respond appropriately to personal and professional limitations.	12.4	Maintain a current list of available referral sources and make referrals in a manner that serves the best interests of the client.	12.4							
13. Maintain professional ethical and legal standards.	13.1	Behave in accordance with AACD ethical guidelines.	13.1							
	13.2	Keep current with case law pertaining to ethical and legal issues in counseling such as duty to warn and maintenance of case records.	13.2							
	13.3	Discriminate between ethical and legal issues in counseling.	13.3							
14. Seek appropriate state and/or national credentialing.	14.1	Know title and title practice laws as they pertain to counseling certification and licensure.	14.1							
	14.2	Be familiar with credentialing organizations at the state (where applicable) and national (e.g., NBCC) levels.	14.2							
	14.3	Know the certification and licensure requirements at the state and national levels.	14.3							
	14.4	Pursue certification and/or licensure whenever possible, in both generic counseling and areas of specialization.	14.4							

2G. MARRIAGE, FAMILY, AND RELATIONSHIP COUNSELING

GOAL STATEMENT: The professional counselor possesses the personality characteristics, knowledge, and skills required of the effective helper, complies with ethical standards and, as appropriate to his or her credentials, understands family dynamics and enhances parenting skills, family patterns, and couple relationships.

COMPETENCIES **The counselor is a skilled professional who is able to:**	PERFORMANCE GUIDELINES **The professional counselor provides evidence of competence by demonstrating the ability to:**		ASSESSMENT	Low 1	2	Average 3	4	High 5	NO	NE
1. Shift the counseling focus from individual dynamics to system dynamics and structure.	1.1	Conceptualize the family or couple as a system and utilize a systemic approach to counseling.	1.1							
	1.2	Understand and respond appropriately to cultural variations of family or couple systems.	1.2							
	1.3	Delineate and map individual and/or subsystem boundaries within the system.	1.3							
	1.4	Engage with and disengage from the system, subsystems, and/or individuals within the system at appropriate times.	1.4							
	1.5	Promote appropriate boundaries within the system.	1.5							
	1.6	Analyze and intervene appropriately in verbal and nonverbal interactional patterns within the system.	1.6							

COMPETENCIES The counselor is a skilled professional who is able to:	PERFORMANCE GUIDELINES The professional counselor provides evidence of competence by demonstrating the ability to:		ASSESSMENT	Low 1	2	Average 3	4	High 5	NO	NE
(Continued) 1. Shift the counseling focus from individual dynamics to system dynamics and structure.	1.7	Analyze and interpret power dynamics within the system.	1.7							
	1.8	Teach ultimate responsibility for individual behaviors within the system.	1.8							
	1.9	Adapt the counselor's preferred individual counseling theory (e.g., Adlerian, behavioral, cognitive, Gestalt, person-centered, transactional analysis) to family, couple, or relationship counseling.	1.9							
2. Be knowledgeable and aware of the family life cycle.	2.1	Identify the current stage of development of the system (family or couple) being counseled.	2.1							
	2.2	Discriminate between normal developmental crises and other systemic issues.	2.2							
	2.3	Recognize multigenerational systemic issues.	2.3							
	2.4	Distinguish between traits of the healthy system and patterns in dysfunctional systems.	2.4							
3. Enact skills specific to parent counseling.	3.1	Engage in counseling with both single and dual parents.	3.1							

				1	2	3	4	5	NO	NE
	3.2	Assist parents in understanding and responding appropriately to normal developmental tasks of children.	3.2							
	3.3	Help parents to establish reasonable behavioral limits for children, and to allow or implement appropriate consequences when those limits are exceeded.	3.3							
	3.4	Help parents to understand the benefits of, and implement, flexibility in parenting.	3.4							
	3.5	Aid parents in adapting to new roles as the family changes to a single-parent or stepfamily configuration.	3.5							
	3.6	Conduct, or direct parents to, formal parenting programs (e.g., STEP, PET, Active Parenting, Filial Therapy).	3.6							
4. Enact skills specific to family counseling.	4.1	Engage in counseling with families of both traditional and nontraditional configurations.	4.1							
	4.2	Utilize a variety of techniques such as escalating stress, relabeling, use of homework, and the use of paradox.	4.2							
	4.3	Facilitate the working through of stresses involving the entire family, such as the death of a child.	4.3							
				Low		Average		High		

COMPETENCIES The counselor is a skilled professional who is able to:	PERFORMANCE GUIDELINES The professional counselor provides evidence of competence by demonstrating the ability to:		ASSESSMENT	Low 1	2	Average 3	4	High 5	NO	NE
5. Enact skills specific to couple counseling.	5.1	Engage in counseling with both traditional and nontraditional couples.	5.1							
	5.2	Engage couples in specific, focused negotiation in the counseling session.	5.2							
	5.3	Help clients work through stresses unique to couple relationships, such as extramarital affairs.	5.3							
	5.4	Conduct divorce therapy if that is the couple's choice.	5.4							
	5.5	Inform the couple about divorce mediation.	5.5							
6. Recognize and address abuse or potential abuse issues in the system.	6.1	Assess the presence of, or potential for, abuse (physical, emotional, sexual, and/or spiritual) within the system.	6.1							
	6.2	Respond appropriately to abuse issues including, under certain circumstances, informing authorities.	6.2							
7. Maintain professional standards.	7.1	Follow ethical standards of professional organizations (e.g., AACD, AAMFT, APA).	7.1							

				1	2	3	4	5	NO	NE
	7.2	Formulate an ethically and legally sound policy regarding confidentiality of individuals within the couple or family system; apprise clients accordingly.	7.2							
	7.3	Network with other professionals for support, consultation, and referral.	7.3							
	7.4	Seek and utilize continuing education.	7.4							
	7.5	Seek certification in areas of specialization (e.g., marriage and family therapy, sexual dysfunction therapy).	7.5							
				Low		Average		High		

2H. MULTICULTURAL AND SPECIFIC POPULATIONS COUNSELING

GOAL STATEMENT: The professional counselor is able to define and recognize the needs of multicultural and specific populations clients and respond to such needs via effective intervention or appropriate referral.

COMPETENCIES **The counselor is a skilled professional who is able to:**	**PERFORMANCE GUIDELINES** **The professional counselor provides evidence of competence by demonstrating the ability to:**		**ASSESSMENT**	**Low** **1**	**2**	**Average** **3**	**4**	**High** **5**	**NO**	**NE**
1. Maintain a multicultural and specific populations perspective of counseling.	1.1	Define and recognize the needs of multicultural and specific populations—persons from any group that is different from the mainstream and has been separated and isolated on the basis of a particular cultural orientation—such as persons from the following groups:	1.1							
	1.1a	African-Americans;	1.1a							
	1.1b	Hispanics;	1.1b							
	1.1c	Asian-Americans;	1.1c							
	1.1d	Native-American Indians;	1.1d							
	1.1e	Euro-Americans;	1.1e							
	1.1f	Women;	1.1f							
	1.1g	Gays and lesbians;	1.1g							

				1 Low	2	3 Average	4	5 High	NO	NE
	1.1h	Persons with disabilities/persons who are physically challenged; and	1.1h							
	1.1i	The aging population (persons over 55).	1.1i							
	1.2	Have an awareness of historical and current sociological and political concerns.	1.2							
	1.3	Maintain ongoing familiarity with culturally relevant issues, concepts, and value systems.	1.3							
2. Understand potential barriers to effective counseling with multicultural and specific populations.	2.1	Recognize the negative impact of the following:	2.1							
	2.1a	The potential for added life stressors that result from being a member of a minority group. The counselor must not neglect the possibility that some client problems may be directly or indirectly caused by the client's minority group status. The counselor must also not overemphasize the impact of minority status on presenting problems to the detriment of gains that could be made from the counseling process.	2.1a							
	2.1b	Transference and countertransference, including the contamination of perception through stereotyping. The counselor must avoid making assumptions about the client prior to checking the accuracy of such assumptions with the client.	2.1b							

COMPETENCIES The counselor is a skilled professional who is able to:	PERFORMANCE GUIDELINES The professional counselor provides evidence of competence by demonstrating the ability to:		ASSESSMENT	Low 1	2	Average 3	4	High 5	NO	NE
(Continued) 2. Understand potential barriers to effective counseling with multicultural and specific populations.	2.1c	History of a client's mistrust of any authority figure that represents the dominant system. The counselor should explain the nature of the counseling process and emphasize the issue of confidentiality.	2.1c							
	2.1d	A client's lack of familiarity (not knowing what to expect) with the counseling process. The counselor can reduce ambiguity through more directive, structured, and goal-oriented counseling approaches.	2.1d							
	2.1e	Imposition of counselor values onto the client as a means of problem resolution. The counselor must attempt to assist the client through the client's own value system.	2.1e							
	2.1f	Lack of knowledge regarding the client's cultural orientation. The counselor should attempt to learn as much as possible about the client's particular culture and determine the degree of assimilation or acculturation that has taken place.	2.1f							
3. Apply theoretical concepts to multicultural and specific populations.	3.1	Have an awareness of culture-specific developmental issues.	3.1							

Competency		Objective		1 Low	2	3 Average	4	5 High	NO	NE
	3.2	Understand the role and function of the family of origin in the cultural context.	3.2							
	3.3	Utilize counseling theory to understand the personality dynamics of multicultural and specific populations.	3.3							
4. Apply skills and strategies to counsel multicultural and other specific populations.	4.1	Have an awareness of common treatment issues or presenting problems specific to the culture of the client. This includes complex concerns that may be masked by the initial concerns.	4.1							
	4.2	Display knowledge and skill regarding individual or group interventions shown to be effective with a particular multicultural or other specific population.	4.2							
	4.3	Display knowledge and skill regarding interventions shown to be effective in working with the family of the multicultural or other specific populations client.	4.3							
	4.4	Maintain ongoing familiarity with effective community agencies and support networks to aid multicultural and specific populations clients and their families.	4.4							
5. Maintain current awareness of multicultural and specific populations counseling and guidance.	5.1	Read professional journals and books regarding the counseling and guidance of multicultural and specific populations.	5.1							

COMPETENCIES The counselor is a skilled professional who is able to:	PERFORMANCE GUIDELINES The professional counselor provides evidence of competence by demonstrating the ability to:		ASSESSMENT	Low 1	2	Average 3	4	High 5	NO	NE
(Continued) 5. Maintain current awareness of multicultural and specific populations counseling and guidance.	5.2	Attend professional conferences, seminars, workshops, or courses of instruction regarding the counseling and guidance of multicultural and special populations.	5.2							
6. Follow established professional ethical guidelines regarding the counseling and guidance of multicultural and specific populations.	6.1	Demonstrate knowledge of the following recognized standards:	6.1							
	6.1a	American Association for Counseling and Development. (1988). *Ethical Standards of the American Association for Counseling and Development.* Alexandria, VA: Author. Cultural factors are specifically addressed in sections:	6.1a							
		A 10. "The member avoids bringing personal issues into the counseling relationship, especially if the potential for harm is present. Through awareness of the negative impact of both racial and sexual stereotyping and discrimination, the counselor guards the individual rights and personal dignity of the client in the counseling relationship."								

				1	2	3	4	5	NO	NE
		B 19. "The member must ensure that members of various ethnic, racial, religious, disability, and socioeconomic groups have equal access to computer applications used to support counseling services and that the content of available computer applications does not discriminate against the groups described above."								
		C 1. "The member must provide specific orientation or information to the examinee(s) prior to and following the test administration so that the results of testing may be placed in proper perspective with other relevant factors. In so doing, the member must recognize the effects of socioeconomic, ethnic, and cultural factors on test scores. It is the member's professional responsibility to use additional unvalidated information carefully in modifying interpretation of the test results."								
		C 12. "The member must proceed with caution when attempting to evaluate and interpret the performance of minority group members or other persons who are not represented in the norm group on which the instrument was standardized."								
				Low		Average		High		

COMPETENCIES The counselor is a skilled professional who is able to:	PERFORMANCE GUIDELINES The professional counselor provides evidence of competence by demonstrating the ability to:		ASSESSMENT	Low 1	2	Average 3	4	High 5	NO	NE
(Continued) 6. Follow established professional ethical guidelines regarding the counseling and guidance of multicultural and specific populations.	6.1b	American Psychological Association. (1990). Ethical principles of psychologists. *American Psychologist*, *45* (3), 390–395. Cultural factors are specifically addressed in principles:	6.1b							
		1:a. "...They provide thorough discussion of the limitations of their data, especially where their work touches on social policy or might be construed to the detriment of persons in specific age, sex, ethnic, socioeconomic, or other social groups..."								
		2:d. "Psychologists recognize differences among people, such as those that might be associated with age, sex, socioeconomic, and ethnic backgrounds. When necessary, they obtain training, experience, or counsel to assure competent service or research relating to such persons."								
		3:b. "As employees or employers, psychologists do not engage in or condone practices that are inhumane or that result in illegal or unjustifiable actions. Such practices include, but are not limited to, those based on considerations of race, handicap, age, gender, sexual preference, religion, or national origin in hiring, promotion, or training."								

Competency		Performance Guideline		1	2	3	4	5	NO	NE
		3:c. "In their professional roles, psychologists avoid any action that will violate or diminish the legal and civil rights of clients or of others who may be affected by their actions."								
7. Maintain ongoing familiarity with local, state, and federal regulations regarding persons from specific populations or multicultural groups.	7.1	Have knowledge regarding significant landmark legislation.	7.1							
	7.2	Help clients to know their civil and legal rights and understand the human and financial costs of exercising their rights.	7.2							

1 2 Low 3 Average 4 5 High   NO NE

2 I. SCHOOL COUNSELING

GOAL STATEMENT: The school counselor possesses the personality characteristics, knowledge, and skills required of the effective helper, complies with ethical standards, and develops, maintains, and provides effective counseling, guidance, consultation, organization, and administration skills and expertise appropriate for a school setting.

COMPETENCIES The counselor is a skilled professional who is able to:	PERFORMANCE GUIDELINES The professional counselor provides evidence of competence by demonstrating the ability to:		ASSESSMENT							
				Low 1	2	Average 3	4	High 5	NO	NE
1. Design and implement a developmental guidance program.	1.1	Understand the psychological, emotional, and physiological development of children and adolescents.	1.1							
	1.2	Stay familiar with national and state models for comprehensive developmental guidance programs, e.g., National Occupational Information Coordinating Committee (NOICC) Standards, Alaska Model, Idaho Model, Missouri Model, Wisconsin Model.	1.2							
	1.3	Assess needs of all students and others served.	1.3							
	1.4	Adapt/devise, implement, and coordinate a comprehensive developmental guidance curriculum that covers the major areas of developmental needs—personal, social, academic, and career.	1.4							

				1	2	3	4	5	NO	NE
	1.5	Adapt the institution's comprehensive developmental guidance model to accommodate specific needs of all student populations, e.g., at-risk, gifted, handicapped, and minorities.	1.5							
	1.6	Develop and coordinate a collaborative team approach to program implementation that involves all members of the guidance team, e.g., students, counselors, parents, teachers, administrators, and community resource persons.	1.6							
	1.7	Plan and conduct classroom guidance activities.	1.7							
	1.8	Assist classroom teachers in implementing guidance activities.	1.8							
	1.9	Assist students in educational and career planning.	1.9							
	1.10	Assist students in transitions between grades or educational levels.	1.10							
	1.11	Inform students, parents, teachers, and administrators about the developmental guidance program and available services.	1.11							
	1.12	Develop a program budget.	1.12							
				Low		Average		High		

COMPETENCIES The counselor is a skilled professional who is able to:	PERFORMANCE GUIDELINES The professional counselor provides evidence of competence by demonstrating the ability to:		ASSESSMENT	Low 1	2	Average 3	4	High 5	NO	NE
2. Manage the guidance program.	2.1	Conduct needs assessments of students, teachers, and parents to determine goals and priorities for the guidance program.	2.1							
	2.2	Plan the school guidance program based on needs assessment.	2.2							
	2.3	Develop evaluation instruments to measure student outcomes related to the guidance program.	2.3							
	2.4	Conduct guidance program evaluation and follow-up studies and share results with school personnel, parents, and students.	2.4							
	2.5	Use results of program evaluation and follow-up studies to improve the guidance program.	2.5							
3. Provide individual and group counseling.	3.1	Counsel individual students in order to meet remedial, preventive, and developmental needs.	3.1							
	3.2	Counsel small groups of students in order to meet remedial, preventive, and developmental needs.	3.2							

				1	2	3	4	5	NO	NE
	3.3	Develop and use effective ways to inform students, staff, and parents about procedures for obtaining individual or group counseling services.	3.3							
	3.4	Respond to students, staff, and parents in crisis.	3.4							
	3.5	Be an advocate for all students.	3.5							
4. Consult with students, teachers, parents, administrators, and other interested individuals.	4.1	Consult with students and parents concerning family situations that affect school attitude and performance.	4.1							
	4.2	Consult with teachers concerning classroom situations that affect school attitude and performance—emphasizing classroom management strategies and the developmental needs of students.	4.2							
	4.3	Consult with teachers, administrators, and staff to meet individual student needs in such areas as attendance, progress, and motivation.	4.3							
	4.4	Conduct parent education groups and individual conferences on specific problems/issues related to normal developmental concerns.	4.4							
				Low		Average		High		

COMPETENCIES The counselor is a skilled professional who is able to:	PERFORMANCE GUIDELINES The professional counselor provides evidence of competence by demonstrating the ability to:		ASSESSMENT	Low 1	2	Average 3	4	High 5	NO	NE
(Continued) 4. Consult with students, teachers, parents, administrators, and other interested individuals.	4.5	Assist teachers in developing curriculum in areas related to counseling, such as career development and psychosocial development.	4.5							
	4.6	Conduct staff development on problem areas that may affect students in schools, such as depression and suicide, attention-deficit hyperactivity disorder, eating disorders, and being at risk of failure.	4.6							
5. Coordinate services available to students, their families, teachers, and school-related personnel.	5.1	Encourage cooperative relationships among and between the school, businesses, and members of the local community.	5.1							
	5.2	Develop an effective referral process for assisting students and school personnel to obtain services of specialized individuals within the school system and agencies within the community.	5.2							
	5.3	Assist special program personnel with student referrals.	5.3							
6. Facilitate the educational and career development of all students.	6.1	Help students understand interrelationships among and between educational, career, and overall human development.	6.1							

				1 Low	2	3 Average	4	5 High	NO	NE
	6.2	Collaborate in identifying, obtaining, and disseminating appropriate educational and career developmental resources.	6.2							
	6.3	Adapt educational and career resources for dissemination to students through infusion in all aspects of the curriculum.	6.3							
	6.4	Encourage teachers to integrate career development activities throughout the curriculum.	6.4							
	6.5	Conduct sessions with students to promote career awareness.	6.5							
	6.6	Provide career and educational opportunity information to students.	6.6							
	6.7	Help students explore postsecondary school education and training opportunities.	6.7							
	6.8	Encourage parents to participate in student planning and decision making.	6.8							
	6.9	Help students develop decision-making skills.	6.9							
	6.10	Facilitate student near-term and long-term educational and career planning and decision making.	6.10							

COMPETENCIES The counselor is a skilled professional who is able to:	PERFORMANCE GUIDELINES The professional counselor provides evidence of competence by demonstrating the ability to:		ASSESSMENT	Low 1	2	Average 3	4	High 5	NO	NE
7. Coordinate student assessment.	7.1	Coordinate the organization, accumulation, and maintenance of student records.	7.1							
	7.2	Assist in the coordination of individual and group testing.	7.2							
	7.3	Administer assessment batteries to assist students in understanding personal interests, abilities, and aptitudes to facilitate making educational, social, and career plans and choices.	7.3							
	7.4	Interpret student information and assessment scores to students, parents, teachers, and administrators.	7.4							
	7.5	Use appraisal data to assist with decisions on student placement.	7.5							
	7.6	Identify students who have special needs.	7.6							
	7.7	Coordinate interviewing and assessing new students and parents prior to enrollment, including a preliminary diagnostic appraisal.	7.7							
	7.8	Review student progress and make reports to parents, teachers, and administrators about student development, adjustment, and achievement.	7.8							

Competency		Indicator		1 Low	2	3 Average	4	5 High	NO	NE
8. Demonstrate regard for professional development and ethical standards.	8.1	Obtain state and national professional credentials.	8.1							
	8.2	Maintain active membership in local, state, and national organizations, such as the American Association for Counseling and Development, the American School Counselors Association, and state and local divisions of AACD and ASCA.	8.2							
	8.3	Abide by established laws and ethical and professional standards.	8.3							
	8.4	Adhere to school board and individual school policies.	8.4							
	8.5	Participate in professional development opportunities on a continuing basis.	8.5							
	8.6	Continue to follow current and innovative strategies and theories in the fields of guidance and counseling.	8.6							

CHAPTER 3

PROGRAM PLANNING, DEVELOPMENT, AND ADMINISTRATION COMPETENCIES

GOAL STATEMENT: The professional counselor possesses the personality characteristics, knowledge, and skills required of the effective helper, complies with ethical standards and, as appropriate to his or her credentials, plans, implements, administers, evaluates, and revises programs for the delivery of counseling and related services.

COMPETENCIES The counselor is a skilled professional who is able to:		**PERFORMANCE GUIDELINES** The professional counselor provides evidence of competence by demonstrating the ability to:	**ASSESSMENT**	Low 1	2	Average 3	4	High 5	NO	NE
1. Establish a program philosophy.	1.1	Identify institutional and community ideals and expectations of the program and its providers.	1.1							
	1.2	Establish program ideals and vision.	1.2							
	1.3	State the program mission.	1.3							
2. Identify populations to be served in the program setting.	2.1	Target such populations as students, parents, teachers, administrators, community representatives, and college representatives in an educational setting.	2.1							
	2.2	Target such populations as community residents, government agencies, churches, and businesses in an agency setting.	2.2							
	2.3	Target such populations as patients, medical staff, administrators, and mental health professionals in a hospital setting.	2.3							

Competency	No.	Task	No.	1 Low	2	3 Average	4	5 High	NO	NE
	2.4	Target such populations as employees and administrators at every level in a business setting.	2.4							
	2.5	Target special populations to be served by the program.	2.5							
3. Be knowledgeable about relevant current literature, trends, and issues.	3.1	Identify issues and factors relevant or potentially relevant to the populations to be served:	3.1							
	3.1a	General developmental needs;	3.1a							
	3.1b	Current public health issues such as drug abuse and sexually transmitted diseases;	3.1b							
	3.1c	Current economic trends; and	3.1c							
	3.1d	Current employment trends.	3.1d							
	3.2	Incorporate legal and ethical considerations into the program development process.	3.2							
4. Conduct needs assessments.	4.1	Initiate needs assessment through consultation interviews with representatives of the populations to be served.	4.1							
	4.2	Design and/or select survey instruments to assess needs of the populations to be served.	4.2							

COMPETENCIES The counselor is a skilled professional who is able to:	PERFORMANCE GUIDELINES The professional counselor provides evidence of competence by demonstrating the ability to:		ASSESSMENT	Low 1	2	Average 3	4	High 5	NO	NE
(Continued) 4. Conduct needs assessments.	4.3	Administer survey instruments in cooperation with other professional personnel.	4.3							
	4.4	Analyze and interpret survey responses.	4.4							
	4.5	Establish priorities among identified population needs.	4.5							
	4.6	Prepare oral and written reports of needs assessment results using terms that can be understood by potential audiences.	4.6							
	4.7	Disseminate results of needs assessments.	4.7							
5. Inventory resources relevant to program planning and implementation.	5.1	Examine existing programs that may serve wholly or in part as models for the program to be developed.	5.1							
	5.2	Identify the capabilities and limitations of the physical facilities in which services will be provided.	5.2							
	5.3	Identify the abilities and limitations of the personnel (salaried, trainee, or volunteer) who will be providing services.	5.3							

				1 Low	2	3 Average	4	5 High	NO	NE
	5.4	Identify the availability and limitations of financial assets for program development and implementation.	5.4							
	5.5	Identify the availability and limitations of time and scheduling considerations in program delivery.	5.5							
	5.6	Identify community, regional, state, national, and other resources that may be exploited to enhance program delivery.	5.6							
	5.7	Maintain a current list of referral sources for use when client needs cannot be met by the program.	5.7							
6. Design a program for delivery of services.	6.1	Integrate relevant data from current literature and trends, needs assessment, and resources in formulating goals for the program (e.g., competence guidelines for staff, logistics of services delivery, and client outcomes).	6.1							
	6.2	Establish policies and procedures for such program components as client intake screening and orientation, client assessment, referral (both into and out of the program), and outreach.	6.2							
	6.3	Develop a format for delivery of direct counseling (and possibly guidance) services to the primary population(s) to be served.	6.3							

COMPETENCIES The counselor is a skilled professional who is able to:	PERFORMANCE GUIDELINES The professional counselor provides evidence of competence by demonstrating the ability to:		ASSESSMENT							
				Low 1	2	Average 3	4	High 5	NO	NE
(Continued) 6. Design a program for delivery of services.	6.4	Develop a format for delivery of ancillary services, such as parent education and staff in-service.	6.4							
7. Implement the program.	7.1	Provide in-service training for staff as needed.	7.1							
	7.2	Order necessary materials.	7.2							
	7.3	Organize personnel and resources for optimal services delivery.	7.3							
	7.4	Inform potential program users of services available.	7.4							
8. Periodically evaluate program effectiveness.	8.1	Identify the criteria on which program effectiveness will be judged.	8.1							
	8.2	Establish an advisory committee of qualified community representatives to provide feedback on program effectiveness and ideas for program improvement.	8.2							
	8.3	Evidence a thorough familiarity with commercial and other professional procedures for evaluating program effectiveness (e.g., checklists, survey instruments, experimental data, observations, and interviews).	8.3							

				1	2	3	4	5	NO	NE
	8.4	Demonstrate skill in using selected evaluation procedures.	8.4							
	8.5	Coordinate program evaluation projects (e.g., delegate responsibilities as appropriate, set deadlines for various stages of the evaluation process, and supervise clerical report preparation).	8.5							
	8.6	Use evaluation results to identify potential areas for refinement and/or revision of program ideals, goals, and services.	8.6							
	8.7	Disseminate evaluation findings to appropriate persons.	8.7							
9. Seek to improve the program.	9.1	Make recommendations to appropriate persons for implementation of program refinement or revision.	9.1							
	9.2	Identify population needs that cannot be met due to limited resources.	9.2							
	9.3	Identify sources of resource enhance-ment.	9.3							
	9.4	Inform those controlling resource enhancement of unmet population needs and resources required to fulfill those needs.	9.4							
				Low		Average		High		

COMPETENCIES The counselor is a skilled professional who is able to:	PERFORMANCE GUIDELINES The professional counselor provides evidence of competence by demonstrating the ability to:		ASSESSMENT							
				Low 1	2	Average 3	4	High 5	NO	NE
(Continued) 9. Seek to improve the program.	9.5	Be aware of opportunities for grant funding and prepare and submit grant funding proposals aimed at resource enhancement.	9.5							
10. Conduct public relations campaigns.	10.1	Identify individuals and groups who might benefit from knowledge of the counseling program, and who might serve as a source of referrals or resource enhancement (e.g., PTAs, school boards, community groups, churches, and businesses).	10.1							
	10.2	Prepare a statement of program ideals, goals, and services that can be adapted to a variety of audiences to whom it may be presented.	10.2							
	10.3	Prepare audiovisual aids to enhance presentations to individuals and groups.	10.3							
	10.4	Schedule presentations at times that are mutually acceptable to the presenter and presentees.	10.4							
	10.5	Present public relations programs in an effective manner.	10.5							

				1 Low	2	3 Average	4	5 High	NO	NE
11. Serve as a consultant/collaborator.	11.1	Consult and collaborate internally with counseling and development team members (e.g., administrators, professionals, paraprofessionals, staff).	11.1							
	11.2	Consult and collaborate with clients and their families, community representatives, public officials, related program providers, and others as appropriate.	11.2							
	11.3	Assist planners (e.g., educational or community) by providing information about the characteristics and needs of the populations served and recommendations about how those needs could best be met.	11.3							
	11.4	Advocate a counseling and development philosophy throughout the work setting and during consultation and collaboration in other settings.	11.4							

CHAPTER 4

LIFE-STYLE AND CAREER DEVELOPMENT COMPETENCIES

GOAL STATEMENT: The professional counselor possesses the personality characteristics, knowledge, and skills required of the effective helper, complies with ethical standards and, as appropriate to his or her credentials, promotes healthy attitudes toward work and career; plans, implements, and evaluates career development programs; and facilitates client career development and mature life planning.

COMPETENCIES The counselor is a skilled professional who is able to:	PERFORMANCE GUIDELINES The professional counselor provides evidence of competence by demonstrating the ability to:		ASSESSMENT	Low 1	2	Average 3	4	High 5	NO	NE
1. Explain career development as a subset of human development.	1.1	Recognize and explain the interrelatedness of career with the balance of life roles.	1.1							
	1.2	Explain life and work roles and their interrelationships, including attention to similarities and differences between one's identity and one's primary vocational function (between who one is and what one does).	1.2							
	1.3	Explain the concepts of and laws regarding equal opportunity and affirmative action in work and career development, emphasizing such areas as age, ethnicity, gender, health, and racial equity in work and career development.	1.3							
	1.4	Explain how technology and change can affect career development.	1.4							

				1 Low	2	3 Average	4	5 High	NO	NE
	1.5	Explain the concept of a work ethic, e.g., the Protestant, personal challenge, or fulfillment ethic.	1.5							
2. Integrate factors related to the world of work.	2.1	Recognize interrelationships of conditions affecting the size and composition of the work force.	2.1							
	2.2	Explain systems for classifying occupations, industries, and skill/ expertise levels required for various occupations.	2.2							
	2.3	Explain global and national economic and industrial patterns and trends in business and industry.	2.3							
	2.4	Identify sources of and help clients exploit labor market information.	2.4							
3. Integrate theories of career/ vocational development and theories of career/vocational choice.	3.1	Explain and discuss strengths and limitations of established theories of career development and career choice.	3.1							
	3.2	Explain and discuss strengths and limitations of emerging theories of career development and career choice.	3.2							

COMPETENCIES The counselor is a skilled professional who is able to:	PERFORMANCE GUIDELINES The professional counselor provides evidence of competence by demonstrating the ability to:		ASSESSMENT	Low 1	2	Average 3	4	High 5	NO	NE
(Continued) 3. Integrate theories of career/vocational development and theories of career/vocational choice.	3.3	Develop and explain a personal theory of career counseling consistent with personal philosophical assumptions, client needs, and agency/institution goals, objectives, and standards, and consonant with agency, AACD, NCDA, and personal ethical standards.	3.3							
4. Plan, design, and implement lifelong career development programs.	4.1	Explain how relevant information, education, training, and professional resources are essential to career development.	4.1							
	4.2	Explain interrelationships of educational, career, leisure, and overall human development across the life span.	4.2							
	4.3	Describe common, lifelong goals of career education, career guidance, and educational and career development programs in terms of institution/agency goals, objectives, and resources.	4.3							
	4.4	Explain the fundamental importance of literacy and communication in career development.	4.4							
	4.5	Explain the fundamental importance of learning to learn as part of one's career development.	4.5							

	No.	Competency	No.	1 Low	2	3 Average	4	5 High	NO	NE
	4.6	Explain the fundamental importance of self-understanding and positive self-concept in life and career development.	4.6							
	4.7	Demonstrate a working knowledge of local, state, and national models, concepts, and strategies for lifelong career education and development, e.g., NOICC Standards, Missouri Model, Wisconsin Model.	4.7							
	4.8	Explain organizational and leadership theories.	4.8							
	4.9	Conduct needs assessment for all populations to be served, including majority, minority, and special needs populations.	4.9							
	4.10	Identify existing institution/agency financial, personnel, and information resources and needs.	4.10							
	4.11	Develop an advisory committee of professional and paraprofessional staff, clients, and community members to plan, implement, and evaluate a career development program.	4.11							

COMPETENCIES The counselor is a skilled professional who is able to:	PERFORMANCE GUIDELINES The professional counselor provides evidence of competence by demonstrating the ability to:		ASSESSMENT	Low 1	2	Average 3	4	High 5	NO	NE
(Continued) 4. Plan, design, and implement lifelong career development programs.	4.12	Develop and implement a career development program for an institution or agency, including provisions for: budget, staffing, facilities, capital equipment, information resources and systems, counseling and placement.	4.12							
	4.13	Suggest career development activities and strategies that can be appropriately infused into the curriculum or other existing institution/agency programs and services.	4.13							
	4.14	Develop formal proposals for funding staffing requirements not met by existing or projected resources.	4.14							
	4.15	Explain, design, and provide career consultation and counseling approaches for business and professional groups through employee assistance programs and human resource development programs.	4.15							
	4.16	Delineate referral procedures for addressing client needs that cannot be met by institutional resources and capabilities.	4.16							

Competency	No.	Objective	No.	1	2	3	4	5	NO	NE
5. Manage career, educational, and personal-social information resources.	5.1	Differentiate data, information, knowledge, and wisdom as they apply to decision making.	5.1							
	5.2	Explain the fundamental importance of and uses for career, educational, and personal-social information in career development and career choice.	5.2							
	5.3	Explain similarities and differences among and between national, state, and local sources of career, educational, and personal-social information.	5.3							
	5.4	Explain concepts of objective and subjective/biographical career information.	5.4							
	5.5	Demonstrate a working knowledge of sources of occupational and educational information materials, such as:	5.5							
	5.5a	Business and industrial firms;	5.5a							
	5.5b	Commercial publishers;	5.5b							
	5.5c1	Governmental sources;	5.5c1							
	5.5c2	U.S. Department of Labor (e.g., DOT, GOE, OOH);	5.5c2							
	5.5c3	National Occupational Information Coordinating Committee (NOICC);	5.5c3							

1 2 3 4 5
Low Average High

NO NE

COMPETENCIES The counselor is a skilled professional who is able to:	PERFORMANCE GUIDELINES The professional counselor provides evidence of competence by demonstrating the ability to:		ASSESSMENT	Low 1	2	Average 3	4	High 5	NO	NE
(Continued) 5. Manage career, educational, and personal-social information resources.	5.5c4	State OICC (SOICC);	5.5c4							
	5.5c5	State career information systems;	5.5c5							
	5.5d	Guides to postsecondary vocational-technical schools, 2-year colleges, and colleges and universities; and	5.5d							
	5.5e	Trade organizations.	5.5e							
	5.6	Demonstrate use of professional guidelines for evaluating information resources.	5.6							
	5.7	Develop a plan, including priorities, for acquiring and organizing career and educational information materials.	5.7							
	5.8	Demonstrate a knowledge of strategies and systems for disseminating career and educational information.	5.8							
	5.9	Explain basic concepts of career development/progression such as career ladders, career lattices, and career paths.	5.9							
	5.10	Evaluate and integrate computer-based information and guidance systems into a career development program.	5.10							

				1	2	3	4	5	NO	NE
	5.11	Conduct liaison with personnel responsible for information resource acquisition and dissemination in the counselor's work setting.	5.11							
	5.12	Work with agency research and development personnel in writing proposals for funding needed resources not funded by current or projected agency budgets.	5.12							
6. Disseminate career and educational information.	6.1	Prepare multimedia presentations of career and educational information.	6.1							
	6.2	Provide general and specific information regarding educational and occupational opportunities, requirements, outlooks, benefits, conditions, and admissions/employment practices for clients, administrators, staff, and significant others.	6.2							
	6.3	Help staff, clients, and significant others recognize and modify career stereotypes.	6.3							
	6.4	Work with institution/agency personnel to assist students/clients in planning and conducting searches for educational and occupational/career information.	6.4							
				Low		Average		High		

COMPETENCIES The counselor is a skilled professional who is able to:	PERFORMANCE GUIDELINES The professional counselor provides evidence of competence by demonstrating the ability to:		ASSESSMENT	Low 1	2	Average 3	4	High 5	NO	NE
7. Identify, select, organize, and provide or arrange for the career and educational components of the agency or institutional appraisal service.	7.1	Evaluate standardized and nonstandardized measurement instruments and procedures in terms of the population(s) served and the career development program goals and objectives of the agency.	7.1							
	7.2	Maintain and use appropriate manuals, forms, and guides to career assessment.	7.2							
	7.3	Identify, select, administer, and interpret standardized measurement/assessment instruments to assess client interests, abilities, values, and personality, or arrange for provision of these activities by appropriate personnel.	7.3							
	7.4	Identify and use nonstandardized assessment procedures such as structured essays, autobiographies, teacher observations, and debriefing questionnaires to facilitate the counselor's and the client's understanding of the client.	7.4							
	7.5	Conduct assessment in strict accordance with personal competence and personal limitations.	7.5							

				1 Low	2	3 Average	4	5 High	NO	NE
8. Organize the career counseling service and provide career counseling and guidance.	8.1	Obtain state and/or national career counseling credentials.	8.1							
	8.2	Effectively use client personal, psycho-logical, and occupational data in career counseling.	8.2							
	8.3	Conduct individual career counseling sessions.	8.3							
	8.4	Conduct group career guidance sessions.	8.4							
	8.5	Understand and explain various decision-making strategies and processes including:	8.5							
	8.5a	Using personal planning strategies and decision models and tools such as goal and priority setting, PERT, study skills, time management techniques, decision trees, sequential decision models, and balance sheet approaches;	8.5a							
	8.5b	Helping clients identify and evaluate alternatives in terms of possible, probable, and desired outcomes;	8.5b							
	8.5c	Helping clients accept responsibility for personal choice and for the conse-quences of personal decisions; and	8.5c							
	8.5d	Helping clients make and evaluate decisions.	8.5d							

COMPETENCIES The counselor is a skilled professional who is able to:	PERFORMANCE GUIDELINES The professional counselor provides evidence of competence by demonstrating the ability to:		ASSESSMENT	Low 1	2	Average 3	4	High 5	NO	NE
(Continued) 8. Organize the career counseling service and provide career counseling and guidance.	8.6	Assess client familiarity with and mastery of decision making and client awareness of common barriers to decision making such as ignorance, avoidance of decisions, fear of irrevocability, fear of failure, and fear of success.	8.6							
9. Organize and manage the educational and career placement service and provide career and educational placement counseling and guidance.	9.1	Demonstrate a working knowledge of career placement counseling and guidance by:	9.1							
	9.1a	Conducting field trips, e.g., to business and industrial sites, technical vocational facilities, and colleges and universities.	9.1a							
	9.1b	Conducting liaison with local and regional employers, especially major area employers and major employers of agency/institutional clients.	9.1b							
	9.2	Establish cooperative working relationships between institutional/agency personnel and the management of local resources such as the state employment service, selected private employment services, employment offices of selected local employers, and employment training programs sponsored by federal, state, and local agencies.	9.2							

				1	2	3	4	5	NO	NE
	9.3	Demonstrate a knowledge of employability skills models and specific techniques.	9.3							
	9.4	Assist clients in making applications and financial plans to attend educational and training institutions and in acquiring employability skills.	9.4							
	9.5	Conduct individual placement sessions.	9.5							
	9.6	Conduct group placement sessions.	9.6							
	9.7	Conduct follow-through/follow-up activities to assess client educational and occupational placements and intervene in the client placement process on a "special-case" basis.	9.7							
10. Identify, assess, and be knowledgeable regarding pertinent legal and ethical factors and their implications for career development.	10.1	Understand and abide by AACD, NCDA, and institutional/agency ethical standards as they relate to all facets of facilitating career development.	10.1							
	10.2	Identify and demonstrate an understanding of common interpretations of pertinent federal, state, and local laws affecting educational and career opportunities, employment, educational and workplace admissions practices, and placement activities.	10.2							
				Low		Average		High		

COMPETENCIES The counselor is a skilled professional who is able to:	PERFORMANCE GUIDELINES The professional counselor provides evidence of competence by demonstrating the ability to:		ASSESSMENT	Low 1	2	Average 3	4	High 5	NO	NE
(Continued) 10. Identify, assess, and be knowledgeable regarding pertinent legal and ethical factors and their implications for career development.	10.3	Identify ethical and legal questions pertinent to the counselor's setting, and become familiar with and obtain written counsel from agency legal advisors regarding these and related questions.	10.3							
	10.4	Educate coworkers, clients, and administrators regarding the counselor's ethical standards.	10.4							
	10.5	Anticipate programmatic ethical concerns by examining and refining the counselor's personal ethical standards in terms of institutional/agency sanctions and goals as well as client needs.	10.5							
11. Evaluate the career development program and use the results to effect program enhancement by recommending institutional/agency improvements.	11.1	Review the findings of appropriate professional research and methodology literature and other descriptions of successful evaluation strategies for determining program effectiveness including:	11.1							
	11.1a	Expert evaluation;	11.1a							
	11.1b	Third-party evaluation; and	11.1b							
	11.1c	Premeasures and postmeasures.	11.1c							

	No.	Item	No.	1	2	3	4	5	NO	NE
	11.2	Coordinate career development program committee work by establishing:	11.2							
	11.2a	Goals to be accomplished by the evaluation;	11.2a							
	11.2b	Specific procedures and timelines for the evaluation; and	11.2b							
	11.2c	Specific responsibilities for carrying out the evaluation.	11.2c							
	11.3	Conduct follow-up studies to obtain data necessary for effective program and agency revisions/improvements by surveying all or randomly selected members of former client populations (e.g., graduates, dropouts, those attending educational institutions, those working).	11.3							
	11.4	Analyze and interpret findings of follow-up studies to staff, clients, and significant others from the community in terms that are understandable to the intended audience.	11.4							
	11.5	Disseminate findings of follow-up studies to the profession and community by all available means.	11.5							
				Low		Average		High		

COMPETENCIES **The counselor is a skilled professional who is able to:**	PERFORMANCE GUIDELINES **The professional counselor provides evidence of competence by demonstrating the ability to:**		ASSESSMENT	Low 1	2	Average 3	4	High 5	NO	NE
(Continued) 11. Evaluate the career development program and use the results to effect program enhancement by recommending institutional/agency improvements.	11.6	Recommend general and specific program and institutional/agency revisions and improvements based on the results of evaluation findings and implications.	11.6							

CHAPTER 5

APPRAISAL COMPETENCIES

GOAL STATEMENT: The professional counselor is able to appraise the characteristics of students and clients, describe the needs and potentialities of individuals, identify individual differences, and provide for recording and disseminating the resultant data.

COMPETENCIES **The counselor is a skilled professional who is able to:**	PERFORMANCE GUIDELINES **The professional counselor provides evidence of competence by demonstrating the ability to:**		ASSESSMENT	Low 1	2	Average 3	4	High 5	NO	NE
1. Understand the basic measurement and evaluation concepts essential in the use of appraisal instruments.	1.1	Apply descriptive statistics to assessment, such as:	1.1							
	1.1a	Derived scores: Grade equivalent scores; Percentile rank; Standard scores;	1.1a							
	1.1b	Tables and graphs: Frequency; Proportion; Percentage;	1.1b							

COMPETENCIES The counselor is a skilled professional who is able to:	PERFORMANCE GUIDELINES The professional counselor provides evidence of competence by demonstrating the ability to:		ASSESSMENT	Low 1	2	Average 3	4	High 5	NO	NE
(Continued) 1. Understand the basic measurement and evaluation concepts essential in the use of appraisal instruments.	1.1c	Measures and characteristics of central tendency: Normal curve and normal distribution; Frequency distribution; Skewness and kurtosis; Mode; Median; Mean;	1.1c							
	1.1d	Measures of variability: Standard deviation; Range; and	1.1d							
	1.1e	Measures of relationship or correlation: Linear; Nonlinear.	1.1e							
	1.2	Apply the concept of validity, including:	1.2							

				1	2	3	4	5	NO	NE
	1.2a	Face validity;	1.2a							
	1.2b	Construct validity;	1.2b							
	1.2c	Content validity;	1.2c							
	1.2d	Criterion-related validity: Predictive validity; Concurrent validity;	1.2d							
	1.2e	Convergent and discriminant validity;	1.2e							
	1.2f	Interpretive validity; and	1.2f							
	1.2g	Incremental validity.	1.2g							
	1.3	Apply the concept of reliability, including:	1.3							
	1.3a	Test-retest reliability;	1.3a							
	1.3b	Alternate forms reliability;	1.3b							
	1.3c	Split-half reliability; and	1.3c							
	1.3d	Internal consistency reliability.	1.3d							
	1.4	Understand the sources of error in test scores.	1.4							
				Low		Average		High		

COMPETENCIES The counselor is a skilled professional who is able to:	PERFORMANCE GUIDELINES The professional counselor provides evidence of competence by demonstrating the ability to:		ASSESSMENT	Low 1	2	Average 3	4	High 5	NO	NE
2. Differentiate between the basic types of assessment.	2.1	Understand criterion-referenced assessment.	2.1							
	2.2	Understand normative-referenced assessment.	2.2							
3. Have an awareness of how to avoid the major sources of assessment error.	3.1	Put the testing process and test results into proper perspective by providing appropriate orientation and information to the client prior to and following test administration.	3.1							
	3.2	Administer tests under designated standardized conditions.	3.2							
	3.3	Utilize the most appropriate assessment device(s) by considering the construct to be measured and the client's emotional, physical, and mental capacities and well-being.	3.3							
	3.4	Apply appropriate norms. This means to:	3.4							
	3.4a	Utilize age-relevant comparisons;	3.4a							
	3.4b	Utilize gender-relevant comparisons;	3.4b							
	3.4c	Utilize socio-economic relevant comparisons; and	3.4c							

Competency	No.	Skill	No.	1 Low	2	3 Average	4	5 High	NO	NE
	3.4d	Recognize the dangers of generalizing to populations not included in the established norm groups.	3.4d							
	3.5	Consider culture-specific values and traditions in assessment and interpretation.	3.5							
	3.6	Know the limitations of the assessment device being utilized.	3.6							
	3.7	Have an awareness of instrumental guidelines for disseminating results, i.e., report in generalizations and ranges and avoid inappropriate applications of stereotypical labels or IQ scores.	3.7							
4. Plan and organize a comprehensive assessment program.	4.1	Select appropriate instruments to measure the construct to be studied. This requires knowledge of tests, inventories, and structured questionnaires, including:	4.1							
	4.1a	Interest;	4.1a							
	4.1b	Aptitude;	4.1b							
	4.1c	Achievement;	4.1c							
	4.1d	Personality; and	4.1d							
	4.1e	Intelligence.	4.1e							

COMPETENCIES The counselor is a skilled professional who is able to:	PERFORMANCE GUIDELINES The professional counselor provides evidence of competence by demonstrating the ability to:		ASSESSMENT	Low 1	2	Average 3	4	High 5	NO	NE
(Continued) 4. Plan and organize a comprehensive assessment program.	4.2	Incorporate nontest data into the overall assessment process, including:	4.2							
	4.2a	Existing records;	4.2a							
	4.2b	Biographies/histories;	4.2b							
	4.2c	Observations;	4.2c							
	4.2d	Structured interviews;	4.2d							
	4.2e	Rating scales; and	4.2e							
	4.2f	Information gathered from family members, teachers, physicians, or referral agencies.	4.2f							
5. Demonstrate competencies in selection, administration, scoring, evaluation, and interpretation of assessment devices.	5.1	Consider as most important the sensitivities and welfare of the client.	5.1							
	5.2	Recognize the limits of professional competence and perform only those functions that are commensurate with professional training and supervision.	5.2							
	5.3	Follow recommended professional ethical guidelines for assessment and evaluation, including:	5.3							

				1	2	3	4	5	NO	NE
	5.3a	Section C: Measurement and evaluation. (1988). In American Association for Counseling and Development. *Ethical standards*. Alexandria, Virginia: American Association for Counseling and Development.	5.3a							
	5.3b	Principle 8: Assessment techniques. (1989). In American Psychological Association. *Ethical principles of psychologists*. Washington, DC: American Psychological Association.	5.3b							
	5.4	Follow legal and ethical codes pertaining to assessment and evaluation that are specific to the state in which the professional practices.	5.4							
	5.5	Have an ongoing familiarity with current knowledge regarding assessment.	5.5							
	5.5a	Maintain updated records and assessment forms.	5.5a							
	5.5b	Utilize the most recent technical information available regarding instrument validity and reliability.	5.5b							
	5.5c	Refer to professional journals that publish recent findings relevant to testing and assessment.	5.5c							
				Low		Average		High		

COMPETENCIES The counselor is a skilled professional who is able to:	PERFORMANCE GUIDELINES The professional counselor provides evidence of competence by demonstrating the ability to:		ASSESSMENT	Low 1	2	Average 3	4	High 5	NO	NE
(Continued) 5. Demonstrate competencies in selection, administration, scoring, evaluation, and interpretation of assessment devices.	5.5d	Refer to professionally recognized published information and standards regarding tests and assessment.	5.5d							
6. Process and make effective use of appraisal data and other relevant information for the purpose of counseling and guidance.	6.1	Prepare charts, tables, graphs, or profiles displaying assessment data.	6.1							
	6.2	Organize appraisal data from several sources into a meaningful format.	6.2							
	6.3	Write an appraisal report that is useful to individuals concerned with the growth and development of the client.	6.3							
	6.4	Conduct effective data interpretation interviews with relevant persons, e.g., clients, students, teachers, parents, administrators, or agency personnel. This involves applying knowledge pertaining to measurement and various assessment devices or techniques to the needs, concerns, and characteristics of individual clients.	6.4							
	6.5	Conduct effective group guidance sessions involving the process of assessment and the use of assessment results.	6.5							

				1 Low	2	3 Average	4	5 High	NO	NE
	6.6	Use appraisal data effectively in arriving at decisions concerning the educational or vocational placement of students and clients.	6.6							
	6.7	Describe the characteristics of gifted, highly creative, and other exceptional individuals and be able to identify such persons accurately through the use of appraisal data and other relevant information.	6.7							
	6.8	Use appraisal data effectively in planning and organizing school curricula or special programs in schools or agencies.	6.8							
	6.9	Make effective use of appraisal data in a case conference for the purpose of enhancing the understanding of an individual student or client.	6.9							

CHAPTER 6

DIAGNOSIS, RECORD-KEEPING, AND REFERRAL COMPETENCIES

GOAL STATEMENT: The professional counselor is able to conceptualize clients based on the assessment categories used in standardized diagnostic systems. The professional counselor maintains current and comprehensive financial, clinical, and other records related to a private, school-based, or community agency counseling practice. The professional counselor assists students, clients, instructional and administrative staff, agency personnel, and parents in the location of and introduction to specialized referral agencies within the community.

COMPETENCIES **The counselor is a skilled professional who is able to:**	**PERFORMANCE GUIDELINES** **The professional counselor provides evidence of competence by demonstrating the ability to:**		**ASSESSMENT**	**Low 1**	**2**	**Average 3**	**4**	**High 5**	**NO**	**NE**
DIAGNOSIS										
1. Accurately and thoroughly conceptualize and diagnose clients based on assessments stemming from standardized nomenclature.	1.1	Understand and appropriately use the diagnostic categories as described in the *Diagnostic and Statistical Manual of Mental Disorders, Third Edition, Revised* (DSM-III-R) such as:	1.1							
	1.1a	Disorders usually first evident in infancy, childhood, or adolescence;	1.1a							
	1.1b	Organic mental syndromes and disorders;	1.1b							
	1.1c	Psychoactive substance use disorders;	1.1c							
	1.1d	Schizophrenia;	1.1d							

	1.1e	Delusional disorder;	1.1e							
	1.1f	Psychotic disorders not elsewhere classified;	1.1f							
	1.1g	Mood disorders;	1.1g							
	1.1h	Anxiety disorders;	1.1h							
	1.1i	Somatoform disorders;	1.1i							
	1.1j	Dissociative disorders;	1.1j							
	1.1k	Sexual disorders;	1.1k							
	1.1l	Sleep disorders;	1.1l							
	1.1m	Factitious disorders;	1.1m							
	1.1n	Impulse control disorders not elsewhere classified;	1.1n							
	1.1o	Adjustment disorder;	1.1o							
	1.1p	Psychological factors affecting the physical condition;	1.1p							
	1.1q	V codes for conditions not attributable to a mental disorder that are a focus of attention or treatment; and	1.1q							
				1 Low	2	3 Average	4	5 High	NO	NE

COMPETENCIES The counselor is a skilled professional who is able to:	PERFORMANCE GUIDELINES The professional counselor provides evidence of competence by demonstrating the ability to:		ASSESSMENT	Low 1	2	Average 3	4	High 5	NO	NE
(Continued) 1. Accurately and thoroughly conceptualize and diagnose clients based on assessments stemming from standardized nomenclature.	1.1r	Additional codes.	1.1r							
	1.2	Define multiaxial evaluation as noted in the DSM-III-R and interrelate a client's personality, physical attributes, psychosocial environment, and level of functioning as demonstrated in the DSM-III-R multiaxial diagnostic system.	1.2							
	1.3	Be aware of reliability and validity factors that contribute to or interfere with accurate assessment and diagnosis.	1.3							
RECORD-KEEPING										
1. Maintain current copies of records required to operate a counseling practice.	1.1	Develop and maintain copies of materials to operate a counseling practice, such as: appointment calendars; intake forms; interview forms; contracts; telephone logs; and information or announcements regarding fees, hours of operation, types of services offered, issues of confidentiality, and credentials of practicing professionals.	1.1							
2. Maintain financial records related to a counseling practice.	2.1	Maintain current and accurate financial records regarding income and expenditures for a counseling practice.	2.1							

Competency		Subcompetency		1	2	3	4	5	NO	NE
3. Maintain clinical records for all persons the counseling practice serves, including clients, significant others, consultees, and referral organizations.	3.1	Develop and maintain accurate and updated clinical records including initial interviews, assessment results, progress notes, and termination notes.	3.1							
	3.2	Ensure confidentiality of all clinical records based on pertinent legal and ethical guidelines.	3.2							
4. Maintain ongoing familiarity with recognized professional standards for record keeping related to a counseling practice.	4.1	Demonstrate knowledge of the following standards as they relate to record keeping in a counseling practice:	4.1							
	4.1a	American Association of Counseling and Development. (1988). *Ethical standards of the American Association for Counseling and Development.* Alexandria, VA: Author.	4.1a							
	4.1b	American Psychological Association. (1990). Ethical principles of psychologists. *American Psychologist*, *45*(3), 390–395.	4.1b							
	4.1c	American Psychological Association. (1981). *Specialty guidelines for the delivery of services.* Washington, DC: Author.	4.1c							
	4.1d	American Psychological Association. (1977). *Standards for providers of psychological services.* Washington, DC: Author.	4.1d							
				Low		**Average**		**High**		

COMPETENCIES The counselor is a skilled professional who is able to:	PERFORMANCE GUIDELINES The professional counselor provides evidence of competence by demonstrating the ability to:		ASSESSMENT	Low 1	2	Average 3	4	High 5	NO	NE
REFERRAL										
1. Identify students, clients, and family systems requiring referral to specialized services within the school system, agencies, or community.	1.1	Possess a working knowledge of the special services within the school district and community and the type of work provided in each service area.	1.1							
	1.2	Evidence adequate knowledge of materials that can be used in screening preschool students and other new students or clients for placement within special assistance units offered by the school district, agency, or community.	1.2							
	1.3	Appropriately understand the capabilities and limitations of school district or agency personnel based on the training, experience, and assignments of special-ized personnel.	1.3							
	1.4	Know the typical behavioral patterns of children and adolescents of various age and maturity levels.	1.4							
	1.5	Know the ranges of normality/abnormality that can be accommodated within institutional or agency teaching/learning/therapeutic programs.	1.5							

				1 Low	2	3 Average	4	5 High	NO	NE
	1.6	Recognize immature speech patterns, articulation problems, and speech impediments for referral to speech-language therapists.	1.6							
	1.7	Recognize indications of visual and other physical impairments for referral to health and medical personnel within the school or community.	1.7							
	1.8	Adequately understand the psychosocial development patterns of children and adolescents. (This implies early referral to school and agency counselors and psychologists and other helping professionals for individuals requiring professional assistance).	1.8							
	1.9	Observe students or clients and confer with teachers, parents, and agency personnel when individual progress decreases.	1.9							
	1.10	Collect data for staff consultation concerning any student or client who is not functioning satisfactorily within the school or agency setting.	1.10							
2. Identify students, clients, and family systems with special and unique referral needs.	2.1	Accurately interpret data obtained from other professional personnel concerning students or clients, individually or in a group setting.	2.1							

COMPETENCIES The counselor is a skilled professional who is able to:	PERFORMANCE GUIDELINES The professional counselor provides evidence of competence by demonstrating the ability to:		ASSESSMENT	Low 1	2	Average 3	4	High 5	NO	NE
(Continued) 2. Identify students, clients, and family systems with special and unique referral needs.	2.2	Prescribe and/or administer further diagnostic measures for students or clients when the need is indicated.	2.2							
	2.3	Recognize factors indicating exceptionality, such as:	2.3							
	2.3a	Creativity;	2.3a							
	2.3b	Intellectual giftedness;	2.3b							
	2.3c	Withdrawn behavior;	2.3c							
	2.3d	Social maladjustment;	2.3d							
	2.3e	Underachievement;	2.3e							
	2.3f	Slow learning;	2.3f							
	2.3g	Retardation;	2.3g							
	2.3h	Severe emotional pathology; and	2.3h							
	2.3i	Attention deficit disorders.	2.3i							
	2.4	Recognize symptoms and characteristics of physical and social/emotional limitations associated with:	2.4							

				1 Low	2	3 Average	4	5 High	NO	NE
	2.4a	Speech handicaps;	2.4a							
	2.4b	Hearing handicaps;	2.4b							
	2.4c	Visual handicaps;	2.4c							
	2.4d	Crippling handicaps; and	2.4d							
	2.4e	Special handicaps.	2.4e							
3. Identify and explain community referral agencies and their services to members of the professional staff, parents, students, and clients.	3.1	Disseminate information about referral agencies and their services to other professional staff members via newsletters, in-service group meetings, and individual contacts.	3.1							
	3.2	Solicit information about possible referral sources from professional staff, service organizations, parents, and others.	3.2							
	3.3	Visit selected referral agencies personally to evaluate their appropriateness as a referral source.	3.3							
	3.4	Arrange for selected professional staff members to visit referral sources being used by school or agency staff.	3.4							
	3.5	Solicit personnel from referral sources to make in-service presentations or give guest lectures about specific services provided to students and clients.	3.5							

COMPETENCIES The counselor is a skilled professional who is able to:	PERFORMANCE GUIDELINES The professional counselor provides evidence of competence by demonstrating the ability to:		ASSESSMENT	Low 1	2	Average 3	4	High 5	NO	NE
(Continued) 3. Identify and explain community referral agencies and their services to members of the professional staff, parents, students, and clients.	3.6	Disseminate referral information to parents, students, and clients.	3.6							
4. Maintain an up-to-date listing of referral sources available within the community.	4.1	Develop a file of available referral sources within the community to include:	4.1							
	4.1a	Name and location of referral source;	4.1a							
	4.1b	Type of services provided;	4.1b							
	4.1c	Criteria for use of services;	4.1c							
	4.1d	Contact person(s); and	4.1d							
	4.1e	Date of information entry.	4.1e							
	4.2	Make regular periodic updates of the referral source file.	4.2							
	4.3	Visit referral agencies to gather additional information to supplement basic entries.	4.3							
5. Exhibit skill in the art of referral to the extent that the person who needs the referral feels comfortable in being referred.	5.1	Exhibit warmth and empathy toward the person being referred.	5.1							

Objective		Competency		1	2	3	4	5	NO	NE
	5.2	Clearly point out possible benefits from referral as well as the handicap incurred by not taking advantage of the referral opportunity.	5.2							
	5.3	Continue to support the client after the referral has been accomplished.	5.3							
	5.4	Make home visitations to assist families with individuals needing referral.	5.4							
	5.5	Present referral information in clear, nontechnical language.	5.5							
6. Facilitate effective referral by means of initiating contacts between referral sources and individuals who have been referred.	6.1	Provide parents, teachers, administrative staff, and students/clients with possible referral sources based on specific need.	6.1							
	6.2	Assist parents, teachers, staff, and students/clients in making the initial contact if requested.	6.2							
	6.3	Visit referral sources for personal contact with resource personnel.	6.3							
	6.4	Conduct case conferences for the dispensation and coordination of data pertinent to specific referrals.	6.4							
				1 Low	2	3 Average	4	5 High	NO	NE

COMPETENCIES **The counselor is a skilled professional who is able to:**	PERFORMANCE GUIDELINES **The professional counselor provides evidence of competence by demonstrating the ability to:**		ASSESSMENT	Low 1	2	Average 3	4	High 5	NO	NE
7. Establish a close working relationship with referral sources commonly used by professional and administrative staff.	7.1	Explain to referral personnel the typical needs of students/clients being referred.	7.1							
	7.2	Provide referral sources with copies of clearly stated policies and procedures for referral that have been established by schools or agencies.	7.2							
	7.3	Solicit from each referral source policies and procedures to be followed by professional staff when using that source.	7.3							
	7.4	Transmit to referral sources appropriate data requested for the effective, efficient handling of referrals.	7.4							
	7.5	Manage referrals in such a way as to avoid duplication of services for clients/students.	7.5							
	7.6	Share with referral sources research conducted by school or agency staff relative to referral needs.	7.6							
	7.7	Express appreciation for services currently provided while pointing to additional needs that require fulfillment.	7.7							

Goal		Competency		1	2	3	4	5	NO	NE
	7.8	Place referral agencies in contact with possible funding sources, personnel, volunteer workers, and others who could be of help.	7.8							
	7.9	Work for joint provision of services, including school, agency, and community cooperation and possible cost sharing.	7.9							
8. Enhance the referral service through follow-up contacts with professional staff and referral sources relative to referral outcomes.	8.1	Establish procedures for transmitting information to and from referral sources.	8.1							
	8.2	Maintain a file of referrals and the disposition of individual cases.	8.2							
	8.3	Transmit data from referral sources to appropriate professional personnel.	8.3							
	8.4	Routinely provide referral sources with follow-up information on individual cases.	8.4							
9. Facilitate follow-up work recommended by community sources as a means of assisting students, clients, and families in working through specific problem areas.	9.1	Assist in the interpretation of data and recommendations transmitted from referral sources.	9.1							
	9.2	Maintain contact with students, clients, and families following referral contacts.	9.2							
	9.3	Provide individual or group counseling experiences as a follow-up to referral source recommendations.	9.3							

1 2 3 4 5
Low Average High

NO NE

COMPETENCIES The counselor is a skilled professional who is able to:	PERFORMANCE GUIDELINES The professional counselor provides evidence of competence by demonstrating the ability to:		ASSESSMENT	Low 1	2	Average 3	4	High 5	NO	NE
(Continued) 9. Facilitate follow-up work recommended by community sources as a means of assisting students, clients, and families in working through specific problem areas.	9.4	Provide consultation to instructional staff members to facilitate follow-through on referral source recommendations in the instructional setting.	9.4							
10. Accept referrals in a competent, professional manner.	10.1	Gather appropriate data on the case being referred.	10.1							
	10.2	Explain initially, with guidelines, the limitations on the types of referrals accepted.	10.2							
	10.3	Develop consent forms to be used in accepting the referral of a minor.	10.3							
	10.4	Delineate procedures for handling the referral, including any follow-up procedures inherent in the process.	10.4							

CHAPTER 7

COUNSELOR SUPERVISION COMPETENCIES

GOAL STATEMENT: The professional counseling supervisor possesses the personality characteristics, knowledge, and skills required of the effective counselor, complies with ethical standards and, as appropriate to his or her credentials, develops and maintains effective supervision skills that will aid counselors in their growth toward their maximum potential.

COMPETENCIES **The counselor is a skilled professional who is able to:**	PERFORMANCE GUIDELINES **The professional counselor provides evidence of competence by demonstrating the ability to:**		ASSESSMENT	Low 1	2	Average 3	4	High 5	NO	NE
1. Teach and apply knowledge of ethical, legal, and regulatory aspects of the profession.	1.1	Inform the counselor of professional codes of ethics (AACD, AAMFT, ASGW, etc.).	1.1							
	1.2	Inform the counselor of legal and regulatory documents and professional accreditation and credentialing standards (state licensure, certification, CACREP, NACC, CCMHC, etc.).	1.2							
	1.3	Inform the counselor of the legal issues that affect counselors and counseling (e.g., confidentiality and privilege, professional disclosure, informed consent, duty to warn, civil and criminal liability).	1.3							
	1.4	Inform the counselor of ethical/legal issues related to the supervisory process (e.g., dual relationships, due process, evaluation, vicarious liability).	1.4							

COMPETENCIES The counselor is a skilled professional who is able to:	PERFORMANCE GUIDELINES The professional counselor provides evidence of competence by demonstrating the ability to:		ASSESSMENT	Low 1	2	Average 3	4	High 5	NO	NE
(Continued) 1. Teach and apply knowledge of ethical, legal, and regulatory aspects of the profession.	1.5	Model appropriate use of ethical and legal standards.	1.5							
2. Apply knowledge of issues related to the supervisory relationship and process.	2.1	Recognize variables that affect the supervisory relationship (e.g., sex roles, ethnicity, supervisory style).	2.1							
	2.2	Establish a supportive environment for the supervisory relationship.	2.2							
	2.3	Deal effectively with supervisee resistance.	2.3							
	2.4	Recognize and clarify the parallel process phenomenon as it develops in the supervisory relationship.	2.4							
	2.5	Use the supervisory relationship as a vehicle for learning about the dynamics of the counseling relationship.	2.5							
	2.6	Display sensitivity to the counselor's anxiety relative to feelings of inadequacy and the evaluative nature of the relationship.	2.6							

				1	2	3	4	5	NO	NE
	2.7	Present an openness of self to feedback from the counselor relative to the effectiveness of supervision.	2.7							
	2.8	Clarify the counselor's personal and professional needs that affect counseling.	2.8							
	2.9	Facilitate counselor exploration of feelings and thoughts experienced during counseling and supervision.	2.9							
3. Apply knowledge of supervision methodology.	3.1	Relate to the counselor in the various roles of: (a) teacher (b) counselor (c) consultant (d) evaluator	3.1							
	3.2	Utilize appropriate supervisory interventions, such as:	3.2							
	3.2a	Role-playing;	3.2a							
	3.2b	Role-reversal;	3.2b							
	3.2c	Live supervision;	3.2c							
				Low		Average		High		

COMPETENCIES The counselor is a skilled professional who is able to:	PERFORMANCE GUIDELINES The professional counselor provides evidence of competence by demonstrating the ability to:		ASSESSMENT	Low 1	2	Average 3	4	High 5	NO	NE
(Continued) 3. Apply knowledge of supervision methodology.	3.2d	Audio/video tape critique;	3.2d							
	3.2e	Group supervision;	3.2e							
	3.2f	Didactic instruction;	3.2f							
	3.2g	Microtraining;	3.2g							
	3.2h	IPR; and	3.2h							
	3.2i	Other ______________.	3.2i							
	3.3	Negotiate a mutual agreement with the counselor regarding training and supervision needed.	3.3							
	3.4	Clarify to the counselor the supervisor's style of supervision.	3.4							
	3.5	Provide equal dimensions of challenge and support.	3.5							
4. Apply knowledge and competence in case management, reporting, recording, and client assessment and evaluation.	4.1	Monitor the use and interpretation of tests and other assessment techniques.	4.1							
	4.2	Assist the counselor in developing report-writing and record-keeping skills.	4.2							

				1	2	3	4	5	NO	NE
	4.3	Assist the counselor in integrating assessment results and observations to establish therapy priorities, set appropriate goals, and/or make appropriate recommendations.	4.3							
	4.4	Assist the counselor in assessing client change.	4.4							
	4.5	Monitor counselor reports to ensure confidentiality of client and supervisory records.	4.5							
	4.6	Assist in developing a networking system and a process for professional referral.	4.6							
5. Apply knowledge of evaluation of counseling performance.	5.1	Specify criteria and procedures for counselor evaluation.	5.1							
	5.2	Identify the counselor's personal and professional strengths and weaknesses.	5.2							
	5.3	Assist the counselor in developing and implementing a self-evaluation plan.	5.3							
	5.4	Behaviorally focus feedback and evaluation related to counseling skills and developmental issues.	5.4							
	5.5	Utilize informal evaluations and standardized rating scales in counselor assessment.	5.5							
				Low		Average		High		

COMPETENCIES The counselor is a skilled professional who is able to:	PERFORMANCE GUIDELINES The professional counselor provides evidence of competence by demonstrating the ability to:		ASSESSMENT	Low 1	2	Average 3	4	High 5	NO	NE
6. Assimilate knowledge of landmark and current counseling and supervision literature and research, and systematically incorporate that knowledge into the supervision process.	6.1.	Understand counseling and supervision literature and research:	6.1							
	6.1a	Historical perspectives;	6.1a							
	6.1b	Current trends and issues; and	6.1b							
	6.1c	Research and its applications.	6.1c							
	6.2	Plan and implement research to evaluate program, counseling, and supervision effectiveness.	6.2							
	6.3	Encourage the counselor to participate in research activities.	6.3							
	6.4	Integrate research findings in supervision and case management.	6.4							
	6.5	Disseminate research findings to other professionals.	6.5							

CHAPTER 8

CONSULTATION COMPETENCIES

GOAL STATEMENT: The professional counselor consults with individuals, groups, institutions, and agencies on guidance, counseling, and developmental needs, concerns, programs, and activities.

COMPETENCIES **The counselor is a skilled professional who is able to:**	PERFORMANCE GUIDELINES **The professional counselor provides evidence of competence by demonstrating the ability to:**		ASSESSMENT	Low 1	2	Average 3	4	High 5	NO	NE
1. Maintain attitudes that form the core conditions necessary for effective consultation relationships.	1.1	Convey unconditional positive regard toward the consultee, as manifested by nonjudgmental, nonpossessive behavior.	1.1							
	1.2	Convey empathy toward the consultee by accurately reflecting the consultee's feelings and subjective reality during the consultation process.	1.2							
	1.3	Convey genuineness toward the consultee by being open, authentic, spontaneous, and flexible; by avoiding defensiveness and game playing.	1.3							
	1.4	Convey a positive perception of self and others.	1.4							
	1.5	Convey a willingness to take personal and professional risks.	1.5							

COMPETENCIES The counselor is a skilled professional who is able to:	PERFORMANCE GUIDELINES The professional counselor provides evidence of competence by demonstrating the ability to:		ASSESSMENT	Low 1	2	Average 3	High 4	5	NO	NE
2. Demonstrate interpersonal skills needed to create and maintain consultation relationships, goals, and desired behavior change.	2.1	Develop rapport with consultee.	2.1							
	2.2	Communicate clear expectations about the consultation relationship by defining goals and desired behavior change.	2.2							
	2.3	Use conflict resolution interventions when necessary.	2.3							
	2.4	Note and respond to the consultee's verbal and nonverbal communication.	2.4							
	2.5	Deal promptly with "here-and-now" issues in the relationship.	2.5							
	2.6	Use appropriate humor.	2.6							
	2.7	Develop and maintain cross-cultural relationships.	2.7							
3. Demonstrate communication skills.	3.1	Nonverbally attend to the consultee.	3.1							
	3.2	Actively listen.	3.2							
	3.3	Express empathy.	3.3							
	3.4	Use questioning strategies to gain more specific information.	3.4							

				1	2	3	4	5	NO	NE
	3.5	Paraphrase the consultee's statements in order to clarify meaning and demonstrate understanding.	3.5							
	3.6	Confront the consultee about discrepancies.	3.6							
	3.7	Provide the consultee with new information that might help facilitate decision making.	3.7							
4. Demonstrate problem-solving skills.	4.1	Set the stage for problem solving by defining consultation as a problem-solving interaction.	4.1							
	4.2	Assess the problem and formulate goals for change.	4.2							
	4.3	Assess the environment and conditions surrounding the problem, noting such components as antecedent events and consequences.	4.3							
	4.4	Gather data about the problem from a variety of sources and analyze the resultant information to diagnose the problem.	4.4							
	4.5	Generate alternative methods of solving the problem, evaluate the different choices, and select the most viable plan.	4.5							
				Low		Average		High		

COMPETENCIES The counselor is a skilled professional who is able to:		PERFORMANCE GUIDELINES The professional counselor provides evidence of competence by demonstrating the ability to:	ASSESSMENT	Low 1	2	Average 3	4	High 5	NO	NE
(Continued) 4. Demonstrate problem-solving skills.	4.6	Assess potential threats to plan implementation and design interventions to capitalize on environmental and consultee strengths.	4.6							
	4.7	Assign responsibilities and arrange for support among individuals and systems in order to facilitate implementation.	4.7							
	4.8	Implement intervention.	4.8							
	4.9	Evaluate process and outcome of problem-solving activities.	4.9							
	4.10	Design formal and informal contracts.	4.10							
5. Demonstrate knowledge base necessary for the process of consultation.	5.1	Demonstrate models of consultation, such as mental health and organizational models.	5.1							
	5.2	Explain organizational theory and the principles and patterns of organizational change.	5.2							
	5.3	Understand group dynamics.	5.3							
	5.4	Understand problem-solving models.	5.4							

Goal		Objective		1 Low	2	3 Average	4	5 High	NO	NE
	5.5	Understand conflict resolution models.	5.5							
	5.6	Understand career development theory.	5.6							
	5.7	Understand referral criteria and techniques.	5.7							
	5.8	Understand personality theories and models of individual change.	5.8							
	5.9	Understand principles of public relations and marketing strategies.	5.9							
	5.10	Understand measurement theory and assessment instrument design.	5.10							
6. Demonstrate skill in working with organizations.	6.1	Establish working relationships with members of the consultee's organization.	6.1							
	6.2	Analyze patterns of interaction occurring in the consultee's organization.	6.2							
	6.3	Provide objective feedback about various aspects of the consultee's organization.	6.3							
	6.4	Gather information from all systems in the consultee's organization.	6.4							
	6.5	Develop organization-wide intervention strategies.	6.5							

COMPETENCIES The counselor is a skilled professional who is able to:	PERFORMANCE GUIDELINES The professional counselor provides evidence of competence by demonstrating the ability to:		ASSESSMENT	Low 1	2	Average 3	4	High 5	NO	NE
(Continued) 6. Demonstrate skill in working with organizations.	6.6	Assess the working atmosphere and climate of the consultee's organization.	6.6							
	6.7	Determine an appropriate use of human resources within the consultee's organization.	6.7							
	6.8	Select an appropriate consultation model, based on the needs of the organization.	6.8							
7. Demonstrate the interactional skills necessary for the consultation process.	7.1	Lead small groups.	7.1							
	7.2	Teach skills.	7.2							
	7.3	Conduct case conferences.	7.3							
	7.4	Interpret and explain assessment data.	7.4							
	7.5	Motivate others.	7.5							
	7.6	Avoid consultation shifting into a counseling relationship even if the consultee desires such a change.	7.6							
	7.7	Recognize consultee resistance and design strategies to combat it.	7.7							
8. Provide consultative expertise collaboratively.	8.1	View consultees as colearners.	8.1							

				1 Low	2	3 Average	4	5 High	NO	NE
	8.2	Conduct consultation sessions based on a concept of cooperative human relationships.	8.2							
	8.3	View self as part of a team approach.	8.3							
9. Interpret and explain concepts and new information effectively.	9.1	Explain such topics as human relationships, group dynamics, human development, and psychological principles applicable to home, school, business, and community settings.	9.1							
	9.2	Gather and present data regarding the characteristics and needs of the consultee population.	9.2							
	9.3	Explain the role and function of the counselor as consultant to potential consultee populations.	9.3							
	9.4	Convey goals and achievements to key personnel in positions of authority, such as executives, principals, and legislators.	9.4							
10. Advocate for individual consultees.	10.1	Facilitate communication among various personnel in consultee organizations.	10.1							
	10.2	Represent the needs of individual consultees to other members of the consultee population.	10.2							

COMPETENCIES The counselor is a skilled professional who is able to:	PERFORMANCE GUIDELINES The professional counselor provides evidence of competence by demonstrating the ability to:		ASSESSMENT	Low 1	2	Average 3	4	High 5	NO	NE
(Continued) 10. Advocate for individual consultees.	10.3	Assist the management of consultee organizations in adopting programs to meet the needs of individual consultees.	10.3							
	10.4	Carry an advocacy role into the community, when necessary.	10.4							
11. Maintain ethical professional behavior.	11.1	Adhere to ethical standards.	11.1							
	11.2	Avoid engaging in consultation beyond the consultant's professional training and expertise.	11.2							
	11.3	Continue professional and personal growth.	11.3							
	11.4	Acknowledge and cope with personal stress inherent in a consultation role.	11.4							
	11.5	Understand legal factors that affect the consultation process.	11.5							

CHAPTER 9

RESEARCH AND EVALUATION COMPETENCIES

GOAL STATEMENT: The professional counselor is able to conduct research, to interpret clearly the implications of research data to professional staff members, parents, students, clients, referral agencies, and community resources, and to use the results of research in counseling, program development, and program revision.

COMPETENCIES **The counselor is a skilled professional who is able to:**	PERFORMANCE GUIDELINES **The professional counselor provides evidence of competence by demonstrating the ability to:**		ASSESSMENT	Low 1	2	Average 3	4	High 5	NO	NE
1. Understand and explain the practical as well as the theoretical principles, concepts, and methods of scientific research and empirical evaluation.	1.1	Define the scientific method as applied to behavioral research.	1.1							
	1.2	Compare and contrast basic and applied research.	1.2							
	1.3	Explain the scientific method of analysis.	1.3							
	1.4	Compare and contrast historical, descriptive, experimental, quasi-experimental, correlational, action, outcome, process, and sociometric research.	1.4							
	1.5	Identify and explain factors that may affect research outcomes, such as:	1.5							

COMPETENCIES The counselor is a skilled professional who is able to:	PERFORMANCE GUIDELINES The professional counselor provides evidence of competence by demonstrating the ability to:		ASSESSMENT	Low 1	2	Average 3	4	High 5	NO	NE
(Continued) 1. Understand and explain the practical as well as the theoretical principles, concepts, and methods of scientific research and empirical evaluation.	1.5a	Sample selection: 1) simple random sampling; 2) stratified random sampling; 3) cluster sampling; 4) systematic random sampling;	1.5a							
	1.5b	Representativeness of the sample;	1.5b							
	1.5c	Participation and cooperation of clients and subjects;	1.5c							
	1.5d	Definition, interaction, and measurement of variables:	1.5d							
	1.5d1	Independent variables;	1.5d1							
	1.5d2	Dependent variables;	1.5d2							
	1.5d3	Confounding variables;	1.5d3							
	1.5d4	Control variables;	1.5d4							
	1.5e	Selection of instruments;	1.5e							
	1.5f	Use of statistical tests;	1.5f							

				1 Low	2	3 Average	4	5 High	NO	NE
	1.5g	Threats to the internal and external validity of research:	1.5g							
	1.5g1	Internal validity:	1.5g1							
	1.5g2	History;	1.5g2							
	1.5g3	Maturation;	1.5g3							
	1.5g4	Testing;	1.5g4							
	1.5g5	Statistical regression;	1.5g5							
	1.5g6	Subject attrition;	1.5g6							
	1.5g7	External validity:	1.5g7							
	1.5g8	Multiple-treatment validity;	1.5g8							
	1.5g9	Interference;	1.5g9							
	1.5g10	Novelty effect;	1.5g10							
	1.5g11	Hawthorne effect;	1.5g11							
	1.5g12	Halo effect; and	1.5g12							
	1.5g13	Experimenter effect.	1.5g13							
2. Prepare a research proposal.	2.1	Select and evaluate a problem for research.	2.1							

COMPETENCIES The counselor is a skilled professional who is able to:	PERFORMANCE GUIDELINES The professional counselor provides evidence of competence by demonstrating the ability to:		ASSESSMENT	Low 1	2	Average 3	4	High 5	NO	NE
(Continued) 2. Prepare a research proposal.	2.2	Explain the procedures used in preparing a research proposal.	2.2							
	2.3	Select an appropriate research proposal title.	2.3							
	2.4	State the research problem clearly.	2.4							
	2.5	Formulate hypotheses:	2.5							
	2.5a	Directional hypotheses;	2.5a							
	2.5b	Null hypotheses; and	2.5b							
	2.5c	Understand Type I and Type II errors.	2.5c							
	2.6	State the background and significance for a proposed research study.	2.6							
	2.7	Define the terms used in the research proposal.	2.7							
	2.8	State the delimitations of a proposed research study.	2.8							
	2.9	State the basic assumptions in a proposed research study.	2.9							

				1	2	3	4	5	NO	NE
				Low		Average		High		
	2.10	Explain the procedures to be used in conducting the study, including how the data will be collected and treated.	2.10							
3. Use the library efficiently for research purposes.	3.1	Locate relevant books, journals, and other research references.	3.1							
	3.2	Use a card catalog or a computer-based, on-line location system.	3.2							
	3.3	Use computer data-base literature search systems.	3.3							
	3.4	Acquire information for research purposes from sources not located in the library through the use of library assistance.	3.4							
4. Conduct a review of professional literature.	4.1	Select studies to be reported.	4.1							
	4.2	Explain procedures for reviewing the literature.	4.2							
	4.3	Efficiently record reference information using the APA citation reference style found in: American Psychological Association. (1983). *Publication manual of the American Psychological Association* (3rd ed.). Washington DC: Author.	4.3							
	4.4	Organize a literature report.	4.4							
	4.5	Write a review of literature.	4.5							

COMPETENCIES The counselor is a skilled professional who is able to:	PERFORMANCE GUIDELINES The professional counselor provides evidence of competence by demonstrating the ability to:		ASSESSMENT	Low 1	2	Average 3	4	High 5	NO	NE
5. Describe and utilize various tools and techniques in research.	5.1	Describe the basic characteristics of questionnaires, checklists, interviews, rating scales and methods, sociometric techniques, and selected tests and inventories.	5.1							
	5.2	Explain the strengths and weaknesses of commonly used research tools and techniques.	5.2							
	5.3	Explain the special applications of various research tools and techniques (e.g., the use of the fact-finding interview, a rating scale, and tests and inventories).	5.3							
	5.4	Evaluate research tools and techniques prior to their use in research. This implies consideration of such factors as validity, reliability, and norms, and making use of standard reference materials.	5.4							
	5.5	Construct instruments and develop methods of measurement when existing tools or techniques are inadequate or unavailable.	5.5							
6. Conduct a research study.	6.1	Use the research proposal as a guide for developing a study.	6.1							

	No.	Competency	No.	1	2	3	4	5	NO	NE
	6.2	Report a review of the literature.	6.2							
	6.3	Define the type of data to be collected, i.e., ratio, ordinal, interval, nominal.	6.3							
	6.4	Explain and conduct sampling procedures.	6.4							
	6.5	Collect and analyze research data.	6.5							
	6.6	Present data graphically for use in research or research reports.	6.6							
	6.7	Use the concept of the normal curve to analyze data.	6.7							
	6.8	Compute descriptive statistics as they apply to the research, such as:	6.8							
	6.8a	Measures of central tendency (including mode, median, and mean);	6.8a							
	6.8b	Measures of variability (including standard deviation and range);	6.8b							
	6.8c	Derived scores (grade equivalent and percentile rank) and standard scores (z-scores, t-scores, and stanines); and	6.8c							
	6.8d	Correlations.	6.8d							
				1 Low	2	3 Average	4	5 High	NO	NE

COMPETENCIES The counselor is a skilled professional who is able to:	PERFORMANCE GUIDELINES The professional counselor provides evidence of competence by demonstrating the ability to:		ASSESSMENT							
				Low 1	2	Average 3	4	High 5	NO	NE
(Continued) 6. Conduct a research study.	6.9	Compute inferential statistics as they apply to the research (including chi-square, t-test, analysis of variance, and multivariate and bivariate statistics).	6.9							
	6.10	Establish confidence intervals.	6.10							
	6.11	Explain and establish levels of significance.	6.11							
	6.12	Draw conclusions based on the research data (findings).	6.12							
	6.13	Write a research report suitable for use by interested individuals, schools, or agencies.	6.13							
7. Apply research knowledge and skills in the field of guidance and counseling.	7.1	Design a variety of research projects that are guidance-and-counseling related. These may include surveys, case studies, correlational studies, experiments, and follow-up studies.	7.1							
	7.2	Explain to interested personnel how the findings of a study can contribute, for example, to the improvement of a course of study, curriculum, program, system, or individual or group intervention.	7.2							

Competency		Objective		1	2	3	4	5	NO	NE
	7.3	Present in writing specific suggestions for changes in procedures, programs, or policies based on research findings.	7.3							
8. Follow recognized professional ethical guidelines and federal, state, institutional, and agency regulations regarding research and measurement activities in guidance and counseling.	8.1	Be familiar with Section D: Research and publication. (1988). In American Association for Counseling and Development. *Ethical standards*. Alexandria, VA: AACD.	8.1							
	8.2	Be familiar with Principle 9: Research with human participants. (1989). In American Psychological Association. *Ethical principles of psychologists*. Washington, DC: APA.	8.2							
	8.3	Be familiar with American Psychological Association. (1982). *Ethical Principles in the conduct of research with human participants*. Washington DC: APA.	8.3							
				1 Low	2	3 Average	4	5 High	NO	NE

SELECTED READINGS

Selected Readings on Personality Characteristics of Professional Counselors

Allen, T. (1967). Effectiveness of counselor trainees as a function of psychological openness. *Journal of Counseling Psychology, 14*, 35–40.

Appell, M. L. (1963). Self-understanding for the guidance counselor. *The Personnel and Guidance Journal, 42*, 143–148.

Association for Counselor Education and Supervision. (1964). The counselor: Professional preparation and role. *The Personnel and Guidance Journal, 42*, 536–541.

Combs, A., Soper, D., Gooding, T., Benton, J., Dickman, J., & Usher, R. (1969). *Florida studies in the helping professions.* Gainesville: University of Florida.

Corey, G., Corey, M. S., & Callanan, P. (1984). *Issues and ethics in the helping professions* (2nd ed.). Monterey, CA: Brooks/Cole.

Corey, M. S., & Corey, G. (1989). *Becoming a helper.* Pacific Grove, CA: Brooks/Cole.

Cottle, W. C., & Lewis, W. W. (1954). Personality characteristics of counselors II. *Journal of Counseling Psychology, 1*, 27–30.

Council for Accreditation of Counseling and Related Education Programs. (1988). *Accreditation procedures manual and application.* Alexandria, VA: Author.

Demos, G., & Zuwaylif, F. H. (1966). Characteristics of effective counselors. *Counselor Education and Supervision, 6*, 163–165.

George, R. L., & Cristiani, T. S. (1990). *Counseling theory and practice* (3rd ed.). Englewood Cliffs, NJ: Prentice-Hall.

Jackson, M., & Thompson, C. L. (1971). Effective counselor: Characteristics and attitudes. *Journal of Counseling Psychology, 18*, 249–254.

National Vocational Guidance Association (1949). *Counselor preparation.* Washington, DC: Author.

Polmantier, P. C. (1966). The personality of the counselor. *The Vocational Guidance Quarterly, 15*, 95–100.

Rogers, C. (1961). *On becoming a person.* Boston: Houghton Mifflin.

Selected Readings on Addiction Counseling

Al-Anon Family Group Headquarters. (1978). *Al-Anon family groups* (rev. ed.). New York: Author.

Alcoholics Anonymous World Services, Inc. (1953). *Twelve steps and twelve traditions.* New York: Author.

Alcoholics Anonymous World Services, Inc. (1976). *Alcoholics Anonymous* (3rd ed.). New York: Author.

Alcoholics Anonymous World Services, Inc. (1986). *AA guidelines for members employed in the alcoholism field.* New York: Author.

Alexander, J. (1941). Freed slaves of drink, now they free others. *Saturday Evening Post, 213*, 9–11.

American Medical Society on Alcoholism and Other Drug Dependencies. (1987). *Acquired immune deficiency syndrome and chemical dependency.* Washington, DC: U. S. Department of Health and Human Services, DHHS Publ. No. (ADM) 87–1513.

American Psychiatric Association. (1987). *Diagnostic and statistical manual of mental disorders* (3rd ed., rev.). Washington, DC: Author.

Arif, A., & Westermeyer, J. (Eds.). (1988). *Manual of drug and alcohol abuse: Guidelines for teaching in medical and health institutions.* New York: Plenum Medical Book Co.

Bean-Bayog, M., & Stimmel, B. (Eds.). *Children of alcoholics: Vol.6, no. 4. Advances in substance abuse.* New York: Haworth.

Beattie, M. (1987). *Codependent no more.* New York: Harper & Row.

Bennett, G., Vourakis, C., & Woolf, D. S. (Eds.). (1983). *Substance abuse: Pharmacologic, developmental and clinical perspectives.* New York: Wiley.

Bissell, L., & Royce, J. E. (1987). *Ethics for addiction professionals.* Center City, MN: Hazelden.

Black, C. (1985). *Repeat after me.* Denver: M.A.C. Printing and Publications Division.

Bradshaw, J. (1988). *Bradshaw on: The family.* Deerfield Beach, FL: Health Communications.
Carroll, C. R. (1989). *Drugs in modern society* (2nd ed.). Dubuque, IA: Wm. C. Brown.
Cohen, S., & Callahan, J. F. (Eds.). (1986). *The diagnosis and treatment of drug and alcohol abuse.* New York: Haworth.
Donovan, D. M., & Marlatt, G. A. (Eds.). (1988). *Assessment of addictive behaviors.* New York: Guilford.
Dupont, R. I., Goldstein, A., & O'Donnell, J. (1979). *Handbook in drug abuse.* Washington, DC: U.S. Government Printing Office.
Dupont, R. L., Jr. (1984). *Getting tough on gateway drugs: A guide for the family.* Washington, DC: American Psychiatric Press.
Elkin, M. (1984). *Families under the influence: Changing alcoholic patterns.* New York: Norton.
Englander-Golden, P., Jackson, J. E., Crane, K., Schwarzkopf, A. B., & Lyle, P. (1989). Communication skills and self-esteem in prevention of destructive behaviors. *Adolescence, 24,* 481–502.
Englander-Golden, P., & Satir, V. (in press). *Say it straight: From compulsions to choices.* Palo Alto, CA: Science & Behavior Books.
Englander-Golden, P., Elconin, J., & Miller, K. J. (1985). Say it straight: Adolescent substance abuse prevention training. *Academic Psychology Bulletin, 7,* 65–79.
Englander-Golden, P., Elconin, J., & Satir, V. (1986). Assertive/leveling communication and empathy in adolescent drug abuse prevention. *Journal of Primary Prevention, 6,* 231–243.
Gallant, D. M. (1987). *Alcoholism: A guide to diagnosis, intervention, and treatment.* New York: Norton.
Girdano, D. A., & Dusek, D. E. (1988). *Drug education: Content and methods* (4th ed.). New York: Random House.
Gitlow, S. E., & Peyser, H. S. (Eds.). (1988). *Alcoholism: A practical treatment guide* (2nd ed.). New York: Grune & Stratton.
Goedde, W. H., & Argawal, D. P. (Eds.). (1987). *Genetics and alcoholism.* New York: Liss.
Gottheil, E. (Ed.). (1987). *Stress and addiction.* New York: Brunner/Mazel.
Jellinek, E. M. (1960). *The disease concept of alcoholism.* New Haven, CT: Hillhouse Press.
Johnson, V. (1980). *I'll quit tomorrow* (rev. ed.). New York: Harper & Row.
Julien, R. M. (1988). *A primer of drug action* (5th ed.). New York: Freeman.
Knott, D. H. (1986). *Alcohol problems: Diagnosis and treatment.* Elmsford, NY: Pergamon.
Lawson, G. W., Ellis, D. C., & Rivers, P. C. (1984). *Essentials of chemical dependency counseling.* Rockville, MD: Aspen Systems.
Lewis, J. A., Dana, R. Q., & Blevins, G. A. (1988). *Substance abuse counseling: An individualized approach.* Belmont, CA: Wadsworth.
Lief, H. I., & Schuster, C. (1988). *Alcohol and sexuality.* Westport, CT: Praeger.
Light, W. H. (1986). *Neurobiology of alcohol abuse.* Springfield, IL: Charles C Thomas.
Meyer, R. E. (Ed.). (1986). *Psychopathology and addictive disorders.* New York: Guilford.
Miletich, J. J. (1988). *Work and alcohol abuse.* Westport, CT: Greenwood Press.
Nathan, P. E. (1988). The addictive personality is the behavior of the addict. *Journal of Consulting and Clinical Psychology, 56,* 183–188.
Radcliffe, A., Rush, P., Sites, C. F., & Cruse, J. (1985). *The pharmer's almanac: Pharmacology of drugs.* Denver: M.A.C., Printing and Publications Division.
Ray, O., & Ksir, C. (1990). *Drugs, society, & human behavior* (5th ed.). St. Louis: Times Mirror/Mosby College Publishing.
Royce, J. E. (1989). *Alcohol problems and alcoholism* (rev. ed.). New York: Free Press.
Russell, M., & Blume, S. (Eds.). (1985). *Children of alcoholics: A review of the literature.* New York: Children of Alcoholics Foundation.
Scanlon, W. F. (1986). *Alcoholism and drug abuse in the workplace.* New York: Praeger.
Schuckit, M. A. (1989). *Drug and alcohol abuse: A clinical guide to diagnosis and treatment* (3rd ed.). New York: Plenum Medical Book Co.
Scott, S. (1985). *Peer pressure reversal: An adult guide to developing a responsible child.* Amherst, MA: Human Resource Development Press.
Scott, S. (1988). *Positive peer groups.* Amherst, MA: Human Resource Development Press.
U. S. Department of Health and Human Services. (1987a). *Alcohol and health.* Rockville, MD: Author.
U. S. Department of Health and Human Services. (1987b). *Drug abuse and drug abuse research.* Rockville, MD: Author.

U.S. Drug Enforcement Administration. (1979). *Controlled substances inventory list.* Washington, DC: Author.
Wegscheider-Cruse, S. (1985). *Alcoholism and the family: A book of readings.* Wernersville, PA: Caron Institute.
Witter, W., & Venturelli, P. (1988). *Drugs and society* (2nd ed.). Boston: Jones and Bartlett.
Woititz, J. (1983). *Adult children of alcoholics.* Deerfield Beach, FL: Health Communications.

Selected Readings on Child and Adolescent Counseling

Axline, V. (1969). *Play therapy.* New York: Ballantine.
Landreth, G. (1982). *Play therapy: Dynamics of the process of counseling with children.* Springfield, IL: Charles C Thomas.
Landreth, G. (1991). *Play therapy: The art of the relationship.* Muncie, IN: Accelerated Development.
Mirkin, M., & Koman, S. (Eds.). (1985). *Handbook of adolescent and family therapy.* New York: Gardner.
Prout, H. T., & Brown, D. (Eds.). (1983). *Counseling and psychotherapy clinic settings.* Tampa, FL: Mariner.
Santrock, J. (1987). *Adolescence: An introduction* (3rd ed.). Dubuque, IA: Wm. C. Brown.
Schaefer, C., & O'Connor, K. (Eds.). (1983). *Handbook of play therapy.* New York: Wiley.
Schaefer, C., & Reid, S. (Eds.). (1986). *Game play: Therapeutic use of childhood games.* New York: Wiley.
Stein, M., & Davis, J. K. (1982). *Therapies for adolescents: Current treatments for problem behaviors.* San Francisco: Jossey-Bass.
Thompson, C., & Rudolph, L. (1988). *Counseling children* (2nd ed.). Pacific Grove, CA: Brooks/Cole.
Walton, F. (1980). *Winning teenagers over in home and school: A manual for parents, teachers, counselors, and principals.* Columbia, SC: Adlerian Child Care Books.

Selected Readings on Community and Mental Health Counseling

Brooks, D. K., Jr., & Weikel, W. J. (1986). History and development of the mental health counseling movement. In A. J. Palmo & W. J. Weikel (Eds.), *Foundations of mental health counseling.* Springfield, IL: Charles C Thomas.
Hershenson, D. B., & Power, P. W. (1987). *Mental health counseling: Theory and practice.* Elmsford, NY: Pergamon Press.
Hoff, L. A. (1989). *People in crisis: Understanding and helping* (3rd ed.). Reading, MA: Addison-Wesley.
Ivey, A. E. (1989). Mental health counseling: A developmental process and profession. *Journal of Mental Health Counseling, 11,* 26–35.
Lewis, J. A., & Lewis, M. D. (1989). *Community counseling.* Pacific Grove, CA: Brooks/Cole.
Palmo, A. J., & Weikel, W. J. (Eds.). (1986). *Foundations of mental health counseling.* Springfield, IL: Charles C Thomas.
Schulberg, H. C., & Killilea, M. (Eds.). (1982). *The modern practice of community mental health.* San Francisco: Jossey-Bass.
Slaikeu, K. A. (1990). *Crisis intervention: A handbook for practice and research* (2nd ed.). Boston: Allyn & Bacon.
Weiner, M. E. (1990). *Human services management: Analysis and applications* (2nd ed.). Belmont, CA: Wadsworth.
West, J. D., Hosie, T. W., & Mackey, J. A. (1988). The counselor's role in mental health: An evaluation. *Counselor Education and Supervision, 27,* 233–239.

Selected Readings on Group Counseling

Association for Specialists in Group Work. (1989). *Ethical guidelines for group counselors.* Alexandria, VA: Author.
Berg, R. C., & Landreth, G. L. (1990). *Group counseling: Concepts and procedures.* Muncie, IN: Accelerated Development.

Corey, M. S., & Corey, G. (1987). *Groups: Process and practice* (3rd ed.). Monterey, CA: Brooks/Cole.

Gazda, G. M. (1989). *Group counseling: A developmental approach* (4th ed.). Boston: Allyn & Bacon.

George, R. L., & Dustin, D. (1987). *Group counseling: Theory and practice.* Englewood Cliffs, NJ: Prentice-Hall.

Jacobs, E. E., Harvill, R. L., & Masson, R. L. (1988). *Group counseling: Strategies and skills.* Monterey, CA: Brooks/Cole.

Seligman, M. (Ed.). (1982). *Group psychotherapy and counseling with special populations.* Baltimore: University Park Press.

Shaffer, J. B. P., & Galinsky, M. D. (1989). *Models of group therapy* (2nd ed.). Englewood Cliffs, NJ: Prentice-Hall.

Yalom, I. D. (1985). *The theory and practice of group psychotherapy* (3rd ed.). New York: Basic Books.

Selected Readings on Higher Education Counseling

Bauer, G. P., & Kobbs, J. C. (1987). *Brief therapy short-term psychodynamic intervention.* Northvale, NJ: Aronson.

Bell, A. P., Weinberg, M. S., & Hammersmith, S.K. (1981). *Sexual preference: Its development in men and women.* Bloomington: Indiana University Press.

Budman, S. H., & Gurman, A. S. (1988). *Theory and practice of brief therapy.* New York: Guilford.

Burkhart, B. R., & Stanton, A. L. (1985). Sexual aggression in acquaintance relationships. In G. Russel (Ed.), *Violence in intimate relationships.* Englewood Cliffs, NJ: Spectrum.

Chickering, A. W. (1969). *Education and identity.* San Francisco: Jossey-Bass.

Drum, D. J., & Lawler, A. C. (1988). *Developmental interventions: Theories, principles, and practice.* Columbus, OH: Merrill.

Erikson, E. H. (1959). *Identity and the life cycle.* New York: International Universities Press.

Erikson, E. H. (1963). *Childhood and society* (2nd ed.). Harmondsworth, England: Penguin Press.

Gallessich, J. (1980). Consultation. In U. Delworth, G. R. Hansen, & Associates (Eds.), *Student services: A handbook for the profession.* San Francisco: Jossey-Bass.

Hoff, L. A. (1984). *People in crisis: Understanding and helping* (2nd ed.) Menlo Park, CA: Addison-Wesley.

Huebner, L. A., & Corazzini, J. G. (1984). Environmental assessment and intervention. In S. D. Brown & R. W. Lent (Eds.), *Handbook of counseling psychology.* New York: Wiley.

Kaiser, L. R. (1978). Campus ecology and campus design. In J. H. Banning (Ed.), *Campus ecology: A perspective for student affairs.* Washington, DC: National Association for Student Personnel Administration.

Kohlberg, L. (1964). Development of moral character and moral ideology. In M. L. Hoffman & L. W. Hoffman (Eds.), *Review of child development research.* New York: Russell Sage Foundation.

Loganbill, C., Hardy, E., & Delworth, U. (1982). Supervision: A conceptual model. *The Counseling Psychologist, 10,* 3–42.

Perry, W. G. (1970). *Forms of intellectual and ethical development in the college years: A scheme.* New York: Holt, Rhinehart & Winston.

Perry, W. G. (1981). Cognitive and ethical growth: The making of meaning. In A. Chickering (Ed.), *The modern American college.* San Francisco: Jossey-Bass.

Piaget, J. (1971). *Biology and knowledge.* Chicago: University of Chicago Press.

Russell, D. E. H. (1984). *Sexual exploration: Rape, child sexual abuse, and workplace harassment.* Beverly Hills, CA: Sage.

Russell, K. R., Crimmings, A. M., & Lent, R. W. (1984). Counselor training and supervision: Theory and research. In S. D. Brown & R. W. Lent (Eds.), *Handbook of counseling psychology.* New York: Wiley.

Shriberg, A., & Brodzinski, F. R. (Eds.). (1984). *Rethinking services for college athletes: New directions for student services.* San Francisco: Jossey-Bass.

Talley, J. E., & Rockwell W. J. K. (Eds.). (1986). *Counseling and psychotherapy with college students: A guide to treatment.* New York: Praeger.

Walsh, W. B. (1973). *Theories of person-environment interaction: Implications for the college student.* Iowa City, IA: The American College Testing Program.

Selected Readings on Individual Counseling

Adler, A. (1963). *The practice and theory of individual psychology.* Patterson, NJ: Littlefield-Adams.

Adler, A. (1964). *Social interest: A challenge to mankind.* New York: Capricorn Books.

Allport, G. (1961). *Pattern and growth in personality.* New York: Holt, Rinehart & Winston.

American Psychiatric Association. (1987). *Diagnostic and statistical manual of mental disorders* (3rd ed., rev.). Washington, DC: Author.

Bandura, A. (1977). Self-efficacy: Toward a unifying theory of behavior change. *Psychological Review, 84,* 191–215.

Beck, A. (1972). *Depression: Causes and treatment.* Philadelphia: University of Pennsylvania Press.

Beck, A. (1976). *Cognitive therapy and the emotional disorders.* New York: International Universities Press.

Belkin, G. S. (1980). *Contemporary psychotherapies.* Chicago: Rand McNally.

Belkin, G. S. (1984). *Introduction to counseling* (2nd ed.). Dubuque, IA: Wm. C. Brown.

Berne, E. (1961). *Transactional analysis in psychotherapy.* New York: Grove Press.

Berne, E. (1964). *Games people play.* New York: Grove Press.

Brammer, L. M., & Shostrom, E. L. (1982). *Therapeutic psychology: Fundamentals of counseling and psychotherapy* (4th ed.). Englewood Cliffs, NJ: Prentice-Hall.

Carkhuff, R. (1969). *Helping and human relations* (Vol. 2). New York: Holt, Rinehart & Winston.

Cormier, W. H., & Cormier, L. S. (1985). *Interviewing strategies for helpers: A guide to assessment, intervention, and evaluation* (2nd ed.). Monterey, CA: Brooks/Cole.

Corsini, R. J., & Wedding, D. (Eds.). (1989). *Current psychotherapies* (4th ed.). Itasca, IL: Peacock.

Dinkmeyer, D. D., Dinkmeyer, D. C., Jr., & Sperry, L. (1979). *Adlerian counseling and psychotherapy.* Monterey, CA: Brooks/Cole.

Dreikurs, R. (1953). *Fundamentals of Adlerian psychology.* Chicago: Alfred Adler Institute.

Dreikurs, R. (1961). The Adlerian approach to therapy. In M. I. Stein (Ed.), *Contemporary psychotherapies.* Glencoe, IL: Free Press.

Egan, G. (1986). *The skilled helper: A systematic approach to effective helping* (3rd ed.). Monterey, CA: Brooks/Cole.

Ellis, A. (1962). *Reason and emotion in psychotherapy.* New York: Lyle Stuart.

Ellis, A. (1971). *Growth through reason.* Palo Alto, CA: Science & Behavior Books.

Ellis, A. (1973). *Humanistic psychotherapy: The rational-emotive approach.* New York: Julian Press and McGraw Hill.

Erikson, E. (1980). *Identity and the life cycle.* New York: Norton.

Frankl, V. (1963). *Man's search for meaning.* New York: Washington Square.

Freud, S. (1924-50). *Collected papers.* London: Imago.

Glasser, E. (1965). *Reality therapy.* New York: Harper & Row.

Glasser, E. (1985). *Control theory.* New York: Harper & Row.

Goulding, M., & Goulding, R. (1979). *Changing lives through redecision therapy.* New York: Brunner/Mazel.

Haley, J. (1973). *Uncommon therapy.* New York: Norton.

Haley, J. (1976). *Problem-solving therapy.* San Francisco: Jossey-Bass.

Horney, K. (1950). *Neurosis and human growth.* New York: Norton.

Ivey, A. E. (1983). *Intentional interviewing and counseling.* Monterey, CA: Brooks/Cole.

Jung, C. G. (1967). *Collected works, (Vol. 5). Symbols of transformation.* Princeton, NJ: Princeton University Press.

Jung, C. G. (1967). *The development of personality. Collected works, (Vol. 17).* Bollingen Series XX. Princeton, NJ: Princeton University Press.

Jung, C. G. (1968). *The archetypes and the collective unconscious. Collected works: Vol. 9, Part I.* Bollingen Series XX. Princeton, NJ: Princeton University Press.

Keirsey, D., & Bates, M. (1984). *Please understand me.* Del Mar, CA: Prometheus Nemesis Book Co.

Korb, M. P., Gorrell, J., & Van De Riet, V. (1989). *Gestalt therapy: Practice and theory* (2nd ed.) New York: Pergamon.

Lazarus, A. (1971). *Behavior therapy and beyond.* New York: McGraw-Hill.

Lazarus, A. (1976). *Multimodal therapy.* New York: Springer.

Maslow, A. (1954). *Motivation and personality.* New York: Harper.
Meichenbaum, D. (1977). *Cognitive behavior modification.* New York: Plenum Press.
Othmer, E., & Othmer, S. C. (1989). *The clinical interview: Using DSM III-R.* Washington, DC: American Psychiatric Association.
Passons, W. R. (1975). *Gestalt approaches in counseling.* New York: Holt, Rinehart & Winston.
Perls, F., Hefferline, R., & Goodman, P. (1951). *Gestalt therapy.* New York: Julian.
Piaget, J. (1929). *The child's conception of the world.* New York: Harcourt Brace.
Rogers, C. R. (1951). *Client-centered therapy.* Boston: Houghton Mifflin.
Rogers, R. (1942). *Counseling and psychotherapy.* Boston: Houghton Mifflin.
Rogers, R. (1961). *On becoming a person.* Boston: Houghton Mifflin.
Rossi, E. L. (Ed.). (1980). *The collected papers of Milton H. Erickson* (4 vols.). New York: Irvington.
Skinner, B. F. (1948). *Science and human behavior.* New York: Macmillan.
Skinner, B. F. (1953). *Walden two.* New York: Macmillan.
Steiner, C. (1971). *Scripts people live.* New York: Grove Press.
Stewart, I., & Joines, V. (1987). *TA today: A new introduction to transactional analysis.* Chapel Hill, NC: Lifespace.
Sullivan, H. S. (1953). *The interpersonal theory of psychiatry.* New York: Norton.
Walen, S., Hauserman, N. M., & Lavin, P. J. (1977). *Clinical guide to behavior therapy.* Baltimore: Williams & Wilkins.
Wolberg, L. R. (1980). *Handbook of short-term psychotherapy.* New York: Thieme-Stratton.
Wolpe, J. (1973). *The practice of behavior therapy.* New York: Pergamon.
Woollams, S., & Brown, M. (1979). *TA: The total handbook of transactional analysis.* Englewood Cliffs, NJ: Prentice-Hall.

Selected Readings on Marriage, Family, and Relationship Counseling

Bader, E., & Pearson, P. T. (1988). *In quest of the mythical mate: A developmental approach to diagnosis and treatment in couples therapy.* New York: Brunner/Mazel.
Barker, R. L. (1984). *Treating couples in crisis.* New York: Free Press.
Beavers, W. R. (1985). *Successful marriage: A family systems approach to couples therapy.* New York: Norton.
Beck, A. T. (1988). *Love is never enough: How couples can overcome misunderstandings, resolve conflicts, and solve relationship problems through cognitive therapy.* New York: Harper & Row.
Becvar, D. S., & Becvar, R. J. (1988). *Family therapy: A systemic integration.* Boston: Allyn & Bacon.
Carter, B., & McGoldrick, M. (Eds.). (1988). *The changing family life cycle: A framework for family therapy* (2nd ed.). New York: Gardner Press.
Curran, D. (1983). *Traits of a healthy family.* San Francisco: Harper & Row.
Duhl, B. S. (1983). *From the inside out and other metaphors.* New York: Brunner/Mazel.
Ellis, A., Sichel, J. L., Yeager, R. J., DiMattia, D. J., & DiGiuseppe, R. (1989). *Rational-emotive couples therapy.* New York: McGraw-Hill.
Fredman, N., & Sherman, R. (1987). *Handbook of measurements for marriage & family therapy.* New York: Brunner/Mazel.
Goldenberg, I., & Goldenberg, H. (1985). *Family therapy: An overview* (2nd ed.). Monterey, CA: Brooks/Cole.
Guerin, J., Jr., Fay, L., Burden, S., & Kautto, J. (1987). *The evaluation and treatment of marital conflicts: A four-stage approach.* New York: Basic Books.
Gurman, A. S. (Ed.). (1985). *Casebook of marital therapy.* New York: Guilford Press.
Gurman, A. S., & Rice, D. G. (1975). *Couples in conflict.* New York: Aronson.
Haynes, J. M., & Haynes, G. L. (1989). *Mediating divorce: Casebook of strategies for successful family negotiations.* San Francisco: Jossey-Bass.
Huber, C. H., & Baruth, L. G. (1981). *Coping with marital conflict: An Adlerian approach to succeeding in marriage.* Champaign, IL: Stipes Publishing.
Jacobson, N. S., & Margolin, G. (1979). *Marital therapy: Strategies based on social learning and behavior exchange priciples.* New York: Brunner/Mazel.

Karpel, M. A. (Ed.). (1986). *Family resources: The hidden partner in family therapy.* New York: Guilford Press.

Kolevzon, M. S. (1988). *The merry-go-rounds of intimate relationships.* North Miami, FL: Kenmarc Press.

Kressel, K. (1985). *The process of divorce: How professionals and couples negotiate settlements.* New York: Basic Books.

L'Abate, L., & McHenry, S. (1983). *Handbook of marital interventions.* New York: Grune & Stratton.

Lewis, J. M., Beavers, W. R., Gossett, J. T., & Phillips, V. A. (1976). *No single thread: Psychological health in family systems.* New York: Brunner/Mazel.

Minuchin, S., & Fishman, H. C. (1981). *Family therapy techniques.* Cambridge, MA: Harvard University Press.

McGoldrick, M., & Gerson, R. (1985). *Genograms in family assessment.* New York: Norton.

Morawetz, A., & Walker, G. (1984). *Brief therapy with single-parent families.* New York: Brunner/Mazel.

O'Hanlon, W. H., & Weiner-Davis, M. (1989). *In search of solutions: A new direction in psychotherapy.* New York: Norton.

Okun, B. F., & Rappaport, L. J. (1980). *Working with families: An introduction to family therapy.* North Scituate, MA: Duxbury Press.

Papp, P. (Ed.). (1977). *Family therapy: Full length case studies.* New York: Gardner Press.

Pittman, F. S., III. (1987). *Turning points: Treating families in transition and crisis.* New York: Norton.

Satir, V. (1983). *Conjoint family therapy.* Palo Alto, CA: Science and Behavior Books.

Sherman R., & Fredman, N. (1986). *Handbook of structured techniques in marriage & family therapy.* New York: Brunner/Mazel.

Stuart, R. B. (1980). *Helping couples change: A social learning approach to marital therapy.* New York: Guilford Press.

Vaughn, D. (1986). *Uncoupling: Turning points in intimate relationships.* New York: Oxford University Press.

Visher, E. B., & Visher, J. B. (1988). *Old loyalties, new ties: Therapeutic strategies with stepfamilies.* New York: Brunner/Mazel.

Wachtel, E. F., & Wachtel, P. L. (1986). *Family dynamics in individual psychotherapy: A guide to clinical strategies.* New York: Guilford Press.

Waring, E. M. (1988). *Enhancing marital intimacy through facilitating cognitive self-disclosure.* New York: Brunner/Mazel.

Wolman, B. B., & Stricker, G. (Eds.). (1983). *Handbook of family and marital therapy.* New York: Plenum Press.

Selected Readings on Multicultural and Special Populations Counseling

Atkinson, D. R., & Hackett, G. (Eds.). (1988). *Counseling non-ethnic American minorities.* Springfield, IL: Charles C Thomas.

Atkinson, D. R., Morten, G., & Sue, D. W. (1983). *Counseling American minorities.* Dubuque, IA: Wm. C. Brown.

Barret, R. L. (1989). Counseling gay men with AIDS: Human dimensions. *Journal of Counseling and Development, 67,* 573–575.

Bass, E., & Davis, L. (1988). *The courage to heal: A Guide for women survivors of child sexual abuse.* New York: Harper & Row.

Carney, C. G., & Kahn, K. B. (1984). Building competencies for effective cross-cultural counseling: A developmental view. *The Counseling Psychologist, 12,* 111–119.

Christensen, C. P. (1989). Cross-cultural awareness development: A conceptual model. *Counselor Education and Supervision, 28,* 270–289.

Comas-Diaz, L., & Griffin, E. (Eds.). (1988). *Clinical guidelines in cross-cultural mental health.* New York: Wiley.

deAnda, D. (1984, March-April). Bicultural socialization: Factors affecting the minority experience. *Social Work,* 101–107.

Dworkin, S. H., & Gutierrez, F. (Eds.). (1989). Gay, lesbian and bisexual issues in counseling [Special issue]. *Journal of Counseling & Development, 68*(1).
Freeman, J. (Ed.). (1989). *Women: A feminist perspective* (4th ed.). Mountain View, CA: Mayfield.
Fretz, B. R. (Ed.). (1985). Cross-cultural counseling [Special issue]. *The Counseling Psychologist, 13.*
Gross, D. (1988). Counseling the elderly: Strategies, procedures, and recommendations. *Counseling and Human Development, 21,* 1–8.
Helms, J. E. (1984). Toward a theoretical explanation of the effects of race on counseling: A black and white model. *The Counseling Psychologist, 12,* 153–165.
Henkin, W. A. (1985). Toward counseling the Japanese in America: A cross-cultural primer. *Journal of Counseling and Development, 63,* 500–503.
Herring, R. D. (1989). The American Native family: Dissolution by coercion. *Journal of Counseling and Development, 17,* 4–13.
Hohenshil, T. H., & Szymanski, E. M. (Eds.). (1989). Counseling persons with disabilities [Special feature]. *Journal of Counseling and Development, 68*(2).
Jones, R. L. (Ed.). (1980). *Black psychology* (2nd ed.). New York: Harper & Row.
Josephson, G. S., & Fong-Beyette, M. L. (1987). Factors assisting female clients' disclosure of incest during counseling. *Journal of Counseling and Development, 65,* 475–478.
Kingdom, M. (1979). Lesbians. *The Counseling Psychologist, 8,* 44–45.
Lafromboise, T. D. (1988). American Indian mental health policy. *American Psychologist, 43,* 388–397.
Landers, S. (1989, November). Programs for Indians draw on tribal customs. *APA Monitor,* p. 32.
Ledray, L. (1986). *Recovering from rape.* New York: Henry Holt.
Lee, C. C. (1982). The school counselor and the black child: Critical roles and functions. *Journal of Non-White Concerns in Personnel and Guidance, 10,* 94–101.
Manio, E. B., & Hall, R. R. (1987). Asian family traditions and their influence in transcultural health care delivery. *Children's Health Care, 15,* 172–177.
Matthews, K. A., & Rodin, J. (1989). Women's changing work roles: Impact on health, family and public policy. *American Psychologist, 44,* 1389–1393.
McNamara, K., & Richard, K. M. (1989). Feminist identity development: Implications for feminist therapy with women. *Journal of Counseling & Development, 68,* 184–189.
Melcher, J. (1988). Psychology in the public forum: Keeping our elderly out of institutions by putting them back in their homes. *American Psychologist, 43,* 643–647.
Melton, G. B. (1989). Public policy and private prejudice: Psychology and law on gay rights. *American Psychologist, 44,* 933–940.
Mitchum, N. T. (1989). Increasing self-esteem in Native-American children. *Elementary School Guidance and Counseling, 23,* 266–270.
Nathanson, R. (1979). Counseling persons with disabilities: Are the feelings, thoughts and behaviors of helping professionals helpful? *The Personnel and Guidance Journal, 58,* 233–237.
Parker, W. M. (1988). Becoming an effective multicultural counselor. *Journal of Counseling and Development, 67,* 93.
Pedersen, P. (Ed.). (1987). *Handbook of cross-cultural counseling and therapy.* New York: Praeger.
Pedersen, P., Lonner, W. J., & Draguns, J. G. (1976). *Counseling across cultures.* Honolulu, HI: University Press of Hawaii.
Ponterotto, J. G. (1987). Counseling Mexican-Americans: A multimodal approach. *Journal of Counseling and Development, 65,* 308–312.
Sanford, L. T., & Donovan, M. E. (1984). *Women and self-esteem.* New York: Penguin Books.
Sue, D. W. (1981). *Counseling the culturally different.* New York: Wiley.
Sue, D. W., & Sue, S. (1972). Counseling Chinese Americans. *The Personnel and Guidance Journal, 50,* 637–644.
Sue, D. W., & Sue, S. (1973). Understanding Asian-Americans: The neglected minority. *The Personnel and Guidance Journal, 51,* 386–389.
Sullivan, T., & Schneider, M. (1987). Development and identity issues in adolescent homosexuality. *Child and Adolescent Social Work, 4,* 13–24.
Wakalee-Lynch, J. (1989, October). Gay and lesbian youths face danger and isolation. *Guidepost.* Alexandria, VA: American Association for Counseling and Development, pp. 1, 4, 7, 16.

Walsh, M. R. (Ed.). (1987). *The psychology of women: Ongoing debates.* New Haven: Yale University Press.
Watson, V. M. (1989, November). Minorities and the legacy of anger. *APA Monitor,* 30–31.
Whiteley, J. (Ed.). (1980). Counseling women III [Special issue]. *The Counseling Psychologist, 8*(1).
Whiteley, J. (Ed.). (1984). Counseling psychology and aging [Special issue]. *The Counseling Psychologist, 12*(2).

Selected Readings on School Counseling

Alaska Department of Education, Office of Adult and Vocational Education. (1989). *Alaska school counseling program guide and pilot project.* Juneau: Alaska Department of Education.
American School Counselor Association Governing Board. (1981). ASCA role statement: The practice of guidance and counseling by school counselors. *The School Counselor, 29,* 7–12.
Bonebrake, C., & Borgers, S. (1984). Counselor role as perceived by counselors and principals. *Elementary School Guidance and Counseling, 18,* 194–199.
Brown, S. T., & Brown, D. (1990). *Designing and implementing a career information center.* Garrett Park, MD: Garrett Park Press.
Burtnett, F., Collison, B., & Segrist, A. (1980). The comprehensive involvement of the school counselor in career education. *Journal of Career Counseling, 7,* 4–21.
Council for Accreditation of Counseling and Related Education Programs. (1988). *Accreditation procedures, manual and application.* Alexandria, VA: Author.
Commission on Precollege Guidance and Counseling. (1986). *Keeping the options open.* New York: College Board.
Committee on School Issues. (1990). *Texas evaluation model for professional school counselors.* Austin, TX: Texas Association for Counseling and Development.
Florida Department of Education, Bureau of Career Development, Division of Vocational, Adult, and Community Education. (1989). *Career development program guide: A guide to the implementation process for career development programs.* Tallahasee: Florida Education Center, Bureau of Career Development.
Helms, B., & Ibrahim, F. (1985). A comparison of counselor and parent perceptions of the role and function of the secondary school counselor. *The School Counselor, 32,* 266–274.
Herbert, D. (Ed.). (1985a). *The role of the school counselor: Elementary level.* Ann Arbor, MI: ERIC Counseling and Personnel Services Clearinghouse. (Information Digest from ERIC/CAPS)
Herbert, D. (Ed.). (1985b). *The role of the school counselor: Middle/junior high level.* Ann Arbor, MI: ERIC Counseling and Personnel Services Clearinghouse. (Information Digest from ERIC/CAPS)
Herbert, D. (Ed.). (1985c). *The role of the school counselor: Secondary level.* Ann Arbor, MI: ERIC Counseling and Personnel Services Clearinghouse. (Information Digest from ERIC/CAPS)
Huey, W., & Remley, T. (Eds.). (1988). *Ethical and legal issues in school counseling.* Alexandria, VA: American School Counselor Association.
Hutchinson, R., Barrick, A., & Groves, M. (1986). Functions of secondary school counselors in the public schools: Ideal and actual. *The School Counselor, 34,* 87–91.
Idaho Department of Public Instruction. (1988). *Idaho comprehensive guidance and counseling program model.* Boise: Author.
Kareen, M., Robinson, E., & Rotter, J. (1985). Coordination activities: A study of perceptions of elementary and middle school counselors. *Elementary School Guidance and Counseling, 20,* 97–104.
Mississippi Bureau of Planning and Policy, Mississippi Bureau of School Improvement, Mississippi Counseling Association. (1989). *Staff development modules for the Mississippi counselor assessment instrument.* Jackson: Mississippi State Department of Education.
Missouri Department of Education, Vocational Special Needs/Guidance Services Section. (undated). *Missouri comprehensive guidance: A model for program development and implementation.* Jefferson: Missouri Department of Education.
National Occupational Information Coordinating Committee. (1989). *The national career development guidelines.* Portland, OR: The Northwest Regional Educational Laboratory.
Northside Independent School District Guidance Department. (1986). *Northside Independent School District comprehensive guidance program framework.* San Antonio: Northside Independent School District.

Oklahoma State Department of Education, Guidance and Counseling Section. (1988). *Building skills for tomorrow: A developmental model.* Oklahoma City: Oklahoma State Department of Education.

Texas Association for Counseling and Development Ad Hoc Committee on School Issues. (1989). Job description of the professional school counselor. *Texas Association for Counselor Education and Supervision Juncture Newsletter, 4*(1), 2–3.

Tennyson, W., Miller, G., Skovholt, T., & Williams, R. (1989). Secondary school counselors: What do they do? What is important? *The School Counselor, 36,* 253–259.

Umansky, D., & Holloway, E. (1984). The counselor as consultant: From model to practice. *The School Counselor, 31,* 329–338.

Wilgus, E., & Shelley, V. (1988). The role of the elementary-school counselor: Teacher perceptions, expectations, and actual functions. *The School Counselor, 35,* 259–266.

Wisconsin Department of Public Instruction. *School counseling programs: A resource and planning guide.* Madison: Author.

Selected Readings on Program Planning, Development, and Administration Competencies

Attkisson, C. C. (Ed.). (1978). *Evaluation of human services programs.* New York: Academic Press.

Austin, M. J., & Hershey, W. E. (Eds.). (1982). *Handbook on mental health administration.* San Francisco: Jossey-Bass.

Ballast, D. L., & Shoemaker, R. L. (1978). *Guidance program development.* Springfield, IL: Charles C Thomas.

Beigel, A., & Levinson, A. (Eds.). *The community mental health center: Strategies and programs.* New York: Basic Books.

Brown, J. A. (1977). *Organizing and evaluating elementary school guidance services: Why, what, and how.* Monterey, CA: Brooks/Cole.

Engels, D. (1980). Looking forward via hindsight: A Rationale for reviewing our ideological roots. *The Personnel and Guidance Journal, 59,* 183–186.

Glaser, D. (1988). *Evaluation research and decision guidance: For correctional, addiction-treatment, mental health, and other people-changing agencies.* New Brunswick, NJ: Transaction.

Gysbers, N. C., & Henderson, P. (1988). *Developing and managing your school guidance program.* Alexandria, VA: American Association for Counseling and Development.

Herr, E. L., & Cramer, S. H. (1988). Systematic planning for career guidance and counseling. In E. L. Herr & S. H. Cramer, *Career guidance and counseling through the life span.* Glenview, IL: Scott Foresman.

Hollister, W. G. (1985). *Alternative services in community mental health: Programs and processes.* Chapel Hill: University of North Carolina.

Popham, W. J. (1975). *Educational evaluation.* Englewood Cliffs, NJ: Prentice-Hall.

Scott, W. R., & Black, B. J. (1986). *The organization of mental health services.* Newbury Park, CA: Sage.

Tolbert, E. L. (1978). *An introduction to guidance.* Boston: Little, Brown.

Walz, G. R. (1988). *Building strong school counseling programs.* Alexandria, VA: American Association for Counseling and Development.

Woolfe, R., Murgatroyd, S., & Rhys, S. (Eds.). (1987). *Guidance and counseling in adult and continuing education: A developmental perspective.* New York: Taylor and Francis.

Yarvis, R. M., & Edwards, D. W. (1982). *Monitoring: The evaluation of mental health programs.* Susan, CA: Pyramid Systems.

Zautra, A., Bachrach, K., & Hess, R. (Eds.). (1983). *Strategies for needs assessment in prevention.* New York: Haworth.

Selected Readings on Life-Style and Career Development Competencies

Bolles, R. N. (1987). *What color is your parachute* (2nd ed.). Berkeley, CA: Ten Speed Press.

Borow, H. (1973). *Man in a world at work.* Boston: Houghton Mifflin.

Borow, H. (1984). The way we were: Reflections on the history of vocational guidance. *The Vocational Guidance Quarterly, 33,* 5–14.

Bradley, L. J. (1990). *Counseling midlife career changers.* Garret Park, MD: Garrett Park Press.
Brown, D., & Brooks, L. (1990). *Career choice and development* (2nd ed.). San Francisco: Jossey-Bass.
Brown, D., & Brooks, L. (1990). *Career counseling techniques.* Boston: Allyn & Bacon.
Crites, J. (1981). *Career counseling, models, methods and materials.* New York: McGraw Hill.
Drummond, B. (Ed.). (1985). Special issue: Unemployment counseling. *Journal of Employment Counseling, 22,* 1–46.
Engels, D., Caulum, D., & Sampson, D. (1984). Computers in counselor education. *Counselor Education and Supervision, 24,* 193–204.
Engels, D., & Muro, J. (1986). Silver to gold: The alchemy, potential and maturing of ACES and CES. *Counselor Education and Supervision, 25,* 289–306.
Engels, D., Sanborn, M., & Schrank, F. (1979). A local approach to identifying biographical literature for vocational exploration. *The Vocational Guidance Quarterly, 28,* 182–186.
Figler, H. E. (1988). *The complete job search handbook* (rev.). New York: Henry Holt.
Flanders, R. (1988). The evolution of the NOICC-SOICC programs: 1977-1987. *Journal of Career Development, 14*(13), 145–168.
Forrest, L., & Mikolaitus, N. (1986). The relational component of identity: An expansion of career development theory. *Career Development Quarterly, 35,* 76–88.
Fredrickson, R. (1982). *Career information.* Englewood Cliffs, NJ: Prentice-Hall.
Gelatt, H. B. (1989). Positive uncertainty: A new decision-making framework for counseling. *Journal of Counseling Psychology, 36,* 252–256.
Gysbers, N. C. (1984). Major trends in career development theories and practice. *The Vocational Guidance Quarterly, 33,* 15–25.
Gysbers, N. C., & Associates. (1984). *Designing careers.* San Francisco: Jossey-Bass.
Gysbers, N. C., & Moore, E. J. (1987). *Career counseling: Skills and techniques for practioners.* Englewood Cliffs, NJ: Prentice-Hall.
Hansen, L. S., & Keirleber, D. L. (1978). Born free: A collaborative consultation model for career development and sex role stereotyping. *The Personnel and Guidance Journal, 56,* 395–399.
Harris-Bowlsbey, J. (1983). The computer and the decider. *The Counseling Psychologist, 11,* 9–14.
Harris-Bowlsbey, J. (1985). The computer and career development: Retrospect and prospect. *Journal of Career Development, 12,* 111–117.
Hartz, J. D. (1978). *Employability inventory: Findings and analysis.* Madison: The Wisconsin Vocational Studies Center, University of Wisconsin.
Herr, E. L., & Cramer, S. H. (1988). *Career guidance and counseling through the life span* (3rd ed.). Glenview, IL: Scott, Foresman.
Holland, J. L. (1973). *Making vocational choices.* Englewood Cliffs, NJ: Prentice-Hall.
Hoppock, R. (1976). *Occupational information* (2nd ed.). New York: McGraw-Hill.
Hoyt, K. (1975). *An introduction to career education.* Washington, DC: U.S. Government Printing Office, p. 39.
Hoyt, K. (1988). The changing workforce: A review of projections—1986 to 2000. *Career Development Quarterly, 37,* 31–39.
Isaacson, I. E. (1986). *Career information in counseling and career development* (3rd ed.). Boston: Allyn & Bacon.
Jaffe, D., & Scott, C. (1988). *Take this job and love it.* New York: Simon & Schuster.
Janis, I. L., & Mann, L. (1977). *Decision making: A logical analysis of conflict, choice and commitment.* New York: Free Press.
Johnston, J., Buescher, K., & Heppner, M. (1988). Computerized career information and guidance systems: Caveat emptor. *Journal of Counseling and Development, 67,* 39–41.
Kapes, J., & Mastie, M. (Eds.). (1988). *A counselor's guide to career assessment instruments* (2nd ed.). Alexandria, VA: National Career Development Association, American Association for Counseling and Development.
Katz, M. (1984). Computer-assisted guidance: A walkthrough with running comments. *Journal of Counseling and Development, 63,* 153–157.
Lewis, J. A., & Lewis, M. D. (1986). *Counseling programs for employees in the workplace.* Monterey, CA: Brooks/Cole.

Leibowitz, Z., & Lea, D. (Eds.). (1990). *Adult career development* (2nd ed.). Alexandria, VA: National Career Development Association.

Mann, L., Beswick, G., Allouache, P., & Ivey, M. (1989). Decision workshops for the improvement of decision-making skills. *Journal of Counseling and Development, 67*, 478–481.

Maze, M. (1984). How to select a computerized guidance system. *Journal of Counseling and Development, 63*, 158–161.

McKinley, B. (1984). Standards of quality in systems of career information. *Journal of Counseling and Development, 63*, 149–152.

National Career Development Association. (1985). Vocational and career counseling competencies. *The Vocational Guidance Quarterly, 24*, 131–134.

National Career Development Association Professional Standards Committee. (1990). *Career counseling competency statements* (Draft). Alexandria, VA: Author.

National Vocational Guidance Association. (1982, June). Vocational/career counseling competencies. *National Vocational Guidance Association Newsletter*, pp. 2–3.

Osipow, S. H. (1983). *Theories of career development* (3rd ed.). Englewood Cliffs, NJ: Prentice-Hall.

Parsons, F. (1909). *Choosing a vocation.* Boston: Houghton Mifflin.

Picchoini, A. P., & Bonk, E. C. (1983). *A comprehensive history of guidance in the United States.* Austin: Texas Personnel and Guidance Association.

Prediger, D. (1981). Getting "ideas" out of the DOT and into vocational guidance. *The Vocational Guidance Quarterly, 29*, 293–306.

Prediger, D. (1981). Mapping occupations and interests: A graphic aid for vocational guidance and research. *The Vocational Guidance Quarterly, 30*, 21–36.

Rose, M. (1981). The feel of a writer's work: An inquiry into the phenomenology of work. *The Vocational Guidance Quarterly, 29*, 236–243.

Rothney, J. W. (1958). *Guidance practice and results.* New York: Harper.

Sampson, J., Shahnasarian, M., & Reardon, R. (1987). Computer-assisted career guidance: A national perspective on the use of DISCOVER and SIGI. *Journal of Counseling and Development, 65*, 416–419.

Savickas, M. L. (1984). Career maturity: The construct and its measurement. *The Vocational Guidance Quarterly, 33*, 232–239.

Savickas, M. L. (1990, January). *Career interventions that create hope.* Unpublished paper presented at the National Conference of the National Career Development Association, Scottsdale, AZ.

Smith, R., Engels, D., & Bonk, E. (1985). The past and future of the National Vocational Guidance Association: History at the crossroads. *Journal of Counseling and Development, 63*, 420–424.

Smith, R., & Waltz, G. (1984). *Counseling and human resource development.* Ann Arbor, MI: Educational Resource Information Clearinghouse/Counseling and Personnel Services Clearinghouse.

Snipes, J., & McDaniels, C. (1981). Theoretical foundations for career information delivery systems. *The Vocational Guidance Quarterly, 29*, 307–314.

Super, D. (1982). The relative importance of work: Models and measures for meaningful data. *The Counseling Psychologist, 10*, 95–103.

Terkel, S. (1975). *Working.* New York: Avon.

Walz, G. R. (1987). The present and the future use of computers by counselors. *Career Planning and Adult Development Journal, 3*, 4–7.

Whiteley, J. (Ed.). (1982). Business and industry [Special issue]. *The Counseling Psychologist, 10*(1), 1–79.

Yost, E. B., & Corbishley, M. A. (1987). *Career counseling: A psychological approach.* San Francisco: Jossey-Bass.

Zunker, V. G. (1981). *Occupational information.* Monterey, CA: Brooks/Cole.

Zunker, V. G. (1989). *Career counseling: Applied concepts of life planning* (3rd ed.). Monterey, CA: Brooks/Cole.

Selected Readings on Appraisal Competencies

American Association for Counseling and Development. (1989, May). The responsibilities of test users. *Guidepost*, pp. 12, 16, 18, 27–28. Alexandria, VA: Author.

American Psychological Association. (1985). *Standards for educational and psychological testing* (rev. ed.) Washington, DC: Author.
Anastasi, A. (1988). *Psychological testing* (6th ed.). New York: Macmillan.
Fretz, B. R. (Ed.). (1990). Testing and assessment [Special issue]. *The Counseling Psychologist, 18*(2).
Joint Committee on Testing Practices. (1988). *Code of fair testing practices in education.* Washington, DC: American Psychological Association.
Mitchell, J. V., Jr. (Ed.). (1985). *The ninth mental measurements yearbook.* Lincoln, NE: The Buros Institute of Mental Measurements.
Sweetland, R. C., & Keyser, D. J. (Eds.). (1984). *Tests.* Kansas City, MO: Test Corporation of America.
Walsh, W. B., & Betz, N. E. (1990). *Tests and assessment* (2nd ed.). Englewood Cliffs, NJ: Prentice-Hall.

Selected Readings on Diagnosis, Record Keeping, and Referral Competencies

American Psychiatric Association. (1987). *Diagnostic and statistical manual of mental disorders* (3rd ed., rev.) (DSM-III-R). Washington, DC: Author.
Baruth, N. E., & Piazza, N. J. (1990). Client record guidelines. *Journal of Counseling & Development., 68,* 313–316.
Berndt, D. J. (1984). Ethical and professional considerations in psychological assessment. *Professional Psychology: Research and Practice, 14,* 580–587.
Blocher, D. H. (1987). *The professional counselor.* New York: Macmillan.
Campbell, R. J. (1981). *Psychiatric dictionary* (5th ed.). New York: Oxford University Press.
Gibson, R. L., & Mitchell, M. H. (1986). *Introduction to counseling and guidance* (2nd ed.). New York: Macmillan.
Goodwin, D. W., & Guze, S. B. (1984). *Psychiatric diagnosis* (3rd ed.). Oxford: Oxford University Press.
Kaplan, H. E., & Sadock, B. J. (1985). *Comprehensive textbook of psychiatry* (4th ed.). Baltimore: Williams & Wilkins.
Keith-Spiegel, P., & Koocher, G. P. (1985). *Ethics in psychology: Professional standards and cases.* New York: Random House.
Kottler, J. A., & Brown, R. W. (1985). *Introduction to therapeutic counseling.* Monterey, CA: Brooks/Cole.
Leon, R. L. (1982). *Psychiatric interviewing: A primer.* New York: Elsevier/North Holland.
Margenau, E. (Ed.) (1990). *The encyclopedic handbook of private practice.* New York: Gardner Press.
Millon, T., & Klerman, G. L. (Eds.). (1986). *Contemporary directions in psychopathology: Toward the DSM-IV.* New York; London: The Guilford Press.
Othmer, E., & Othmer, S. C. (1989). *The clinical interview using DSM-III-R.* Washington, DC: American Psychiatric Press.
Spitzer, R. L., Gibbon, M., Skodol, A. E., Williams, J. B., & First, M. B. (1989). *DSM-III-R diagnostic and statistical manual of mental disorders* (rev. ed.). Washington, DC: American Psychiatric Press.

Selected Readings on Counselor Supervision Competencies

Association for Counselor Education and Supervision. (1989, Spring). Standards for counseling supervisors. *ACES Spectrum,* pp. 7–10.
Association for Counselor Education and Supervision. (1990, Spring). Ethical standards for counselor supervisors. *ACES Spectrum.,* pp. 12–15.
Borders, L. D., & Leddick, G. R. (1987). *Handbook for counseling supervision.* Alexandria, VA: American Association for Counseling and Development.
Bradley, L. J. (1989). *Counselor supervision: Principles, process, and practice* (2nd ed.). Muncie, IN: Accelerated Development.
Falvey, J. E. (1987). *Handbook of administrative supervision.* Alexandria, VA: Association for Counselor Education and Supervision.

Hendrickson, D. E., & Krause, F. H. (Eds.). (1972). *Counseling and psychotherapy: Training and supervision.* Columbus, OH: Merrill.
Hess, A. K. (Ed.). (1980). *Psychotherapy supervision: Theory, research, and practice.* New York: Wiley.
Kell, B. L., & Mueller, W. J. (1966). *Impact and change: A study of counseling relationships.* New York: Appleton-Century-Crofts.
Mueller, W. J., & Kell, B. L. (1972). *Coping with conflict: Supervising counselors and psychotherapists.* New York: Appleton-Century-Crofts.
Stoltenberg, C. D., & Delworth, U. (1987). *Supervising counselors and therapists: A developmental approach.* San Francisco: Jossey-Bass.
Whiteley, J. M. (Ed.). (1982). Supervision in counseling I [Special issue]. *The Counseling Psychologist, 10*(1).
Whiteley, J. M. (Ed.). (1983). Supervision in counseling II [Special issue]. *The Counseling Psychologist, 11*(1).

Selected Readings on Consultation Competencies

Alpert, J., & Meyers, J. (Eds.). (1983). *Training in consultation.* Springfield, IL: Charles C Thomas.
Brown, D., Kurpius, D., & Morris, J. (1988). *Handbook of consultation with individuals and small groups.* Alexandria, VA: Association for Counselor Education and Supervision.
Brown, D., Pryzwansky, W., & Schulte, A. (1987). *Psychological consultation: Introduction to theory and practice.* Boston: Allyn & Bacon.
Committee on School Issues (1990). *Texas evaluation model for professional school counselors.* Austin, TX: Texas Association for Counseling and Development.
Conoley, J., & Conoley, C. (1982). *School consultation: A guide to practice and training.* New York: Pergamon Press.
Dougherty, A. M. (1990). *Consultation: Practice and perspectives.* Belmont, CA: Brooks/Cole.
Fuqua, D., & Newman, J. (1985). Individual consultation. *The Counseling Psychologist, 13,* 390–395.
Gallessich, J. (1982). *The profession and practice of consultation.* San Francisco: Jossey-Bass.
Kirby, J. (1985). *Consultation: Practice and practitioner.* Muncie, IN: Accelerated Development.
Kurpius, D. (1985). Consultation interventions: Success, failures and proposals. *The Counseling Psychologist, 13,* 368–389.
Kurpius, D., & Brown, D. (Eds.). (1988). *Handbook of consultation: An intervention for advocacy and outreach.* Alexandria, VA: Association for Counselor Education and Supervision.
Lippitt, G., & Lippitt, R. (1986). *The consulting process in action.* San Diego: University Associates.
Mannino, F., Tricket, E., Shore, M., Kidder, M., & Levin, G. (Eds.). (1986). *Handbook of mental health consultation.* Rockville, MD: National Institute for Mental Health.
National Vocational Guidance Association. (1982, June). *Vocational/career counseling competencies continued.* Washington, DC: National Vocational Guidance Association Newsletter.
Parsons, R., & Meyers, J. (1984). *Developing consultation skills.* San Francisco: Jossey-Bass.
Schmidt, J., & Medl, W. (1983). Six magic steps of consulting. *The School Counselor, 30,* 212–216.
Ulmansky, D., & Holloway, E. (1984). The counselor as consultant: From model to practice. *The School Counselor, 31,* 329–338.

Selected Readings on Research and Evaluation Competencies

Appelbaum, P. S., & Rosenbaum, A. (1989). Tarasoff and the researcher: Does the duty to protect apply in the research setting? *American Psychologist, 44,* 885–894.
Brigham, T. A. (1989). On the importance of recognizing the difference between experiments and correlational studies. *American Psychologist, 44,* 1077–1078.
Denmark, F., Russo, N. F., Frieze, I. H., & Sechzer, J. A. (1988). Guidelines for avoiding sexism in psychological research. *American Psychologist, 43,* 582–585.
Dorn, F. J. (1985). Developing your publication potential and copyrighting confidence. *Journal of Counseling and Development, 63,* 512–514.
Drew, C. J., & Hardman, M. L. (1985). *Designing and conducting behavioral research.* New York: Pergamon.
Hoshmand, L. (1989). Alternate research paradigms: A review and teaching proposal. *The Counseling Psychologist, 17,* 3–79.

Martin, D., & Martin, M. (1989). Bridging the gap between research and practice. *Journal of Counseling and Development, 67,* 491–492.
Melton, G. B., & Gray, J. N. (1988). Ethical dilemmas in AIDS research. *American Psychologist, 43,* 60–64.
Osberg, T. M. (1989). Self-report reconsidered: A further look at its advantages as an assessment technique. *Journal of Counseling & Development, 68,* 111–113.
Rosen, G. M. (1987). Self-help treatment books and the commercialization of psychotherapy. *American Psychologist, 42,* 46–51.
Scarr, S. (1988). Race and gender as psychological variables. *American Psychologist, 43,* 56–59.
Seiber, J. E., & Stanley, B. (1988). Ethical and professional dimensions of socially sensitive research. *American Psychologist, 43,* 49–55.
Strupp, H. H. (1989). Psychotherapy: Can the practitioner learn from the researcher? *American Psychologist, 44,* 717–724.
Tracy, T. (1985). Single-case research: An added tool for counselors and supervisors. *Counselor Education and Supervision, 23,* 185–195.
VandenBos, G. R. (Ed.). (1986). Psychotherapy research [Special issue]. *American Psychologist, 41*(2).
Whiteley, J. M. (Ed.). (1980). Research in counseling psychology [Special issue]. *The Counseling Psychologist, 8*(3).
Whiteley, J. M. (Ed.). (1982). Research in counseling psychology II [Special issue]. *The Counseling Psychologist, 10*(4).
Wilcoxon, S. A. (1989). He/she/they/it?: Implied sexism in speech and print. *Journal of Counseling & Development, 68,* 114–116.
Winston, R. B. (1985). Suggested procedure for determining order of authorship in research publications. *Journal of Counseling and Development, 63,* 515–518.